KT-212-995

Marie M. Fortune, MDiv, DHLit
W. Merle Longwood, PhD
Editors

Sexual Abuse in the Catholic Church: Trusting the Clergy?

Sexual Abuse in the Catholic Church: Trusting the Clergy?
has been co-published simultaneously as *Journal of Religion & Abuse,* Volume 5, Number 3 2003.

Pre-publication
REVIEWS,
COMMENTARIES,
EVALUATIONS . . .

"**A** REMARKABLE ACHIEVE-MENT. . . Brings together a number of reasoned multidisciplinary voices. . . . Adds much-needed insight and clarity to this challenging problem. Thoughtful and data-driven. . . . Anyone interested in the topic will benefit from reading this book."

Thomas G. Plante, PhD, ABPP
Professor, Psychology Department
Editor of Sin Against the Innocents: Sexual Abuse by Priests and the Role of the Catholic Church *and* Bless Me Father for I Have Sinned: Perspectives on Sexual Abuse Committed by Roman Catholic Priests

More Pre-publication
REVIEWS, COMMENTARIES, EVALUATIONS. . .

" **A** RICH RESOURCE for individuals and church communities coming to terms with the realities of this violence and betrayal in their own lives. . . . A VALUABLE GUIDE FOR STUDENTS in its analysis of church life, governance, and pastoral ethics. I warmly commend this book to the church at large–Catholic, Protestant, and Orthodox

Rev. Dr. Andrew Dutney
Senior Lecturer
Flinders University
Principal
Parkin-Wesley College
Director
The Centre for Theology,
Science & Culture

The Haworth Pastoral Press®
An Imprint of The Haworth Press, Inc.

New York • London • Victoria (AU)
www.HaworthPress.com

Sexual Abuse in the Catholic Church: Trusting the Clergy?

Sexual Abuse in the Catholic Church: Trusting the Clergy? has been co-published simultaneously as *Journal of Religion & Abuse,* Volume 5, Number 3 2003.

The *Journal of Religion & Abuse* Monographic "Separates"

Below is a list of "separates," which in serials librarianship means a special issue simultaneously published as a special journal issue or double-issue *and* as a "separate" hardbound monograph. (This is a format which we also call a "DocuSerial.")

"Separates" are published because specialized libraries or professionals may wish to purchase a specific thematic issue by itself in a format which can be separately cataloged and shelved, as opposed to purchasing the journal on an on-going basis. Faculty members may also more easily consider a "separate" for classroom adoption.

"Separates" are carefully classified separately with the major book jobbers so that the journal tie-in can be noted on new book order slips to avoid duplicate purchasing.

You may wish to visit Haworth's website at . . .

http://www.HaworthPress.com

. . . to search our online catalog for complete tables of contents of these separates and related publications.

You may also call 1-800-HAWORTH (outside US/Canada: 607-722-5857). or Fax 1-800-895-0582 (outside US/Canada: 607-771-0012), or e-mail at:

docdelivery@haworthpress.com

Sexual Abuse in the Catholic Church: Trusting the Clergy?, edited by Rev. Marie M. Fortune, MDiv, DHLit, and W. Merle Longwood, PhD (Vol. 5, No. 3, 2003). *"A REMARKABLE ACHIEVEMENT. . . Brings together a number of reasoned multidisciplinary voices. . . . Adds much-needed insight and clarity to this challenging problem. Thoughtful and data-driven. . . . Anyone interested in the topic will benefit from reading this book." (Thomas G. Plante, PhD, ABPP. Professor, Psychology Department, Santa Clara University)*

Forgiveness and Abuse: Jewish and Christian Reflections, edited by Marie M. Fortune, MDiv, DHLit, and Joretta L. Marshall, PhD. MDiv, (Vol. 4, No. 4, 2002). *"PROFOUNDLY SIGNIFICANT. . . . Uncovering both the misconceptions and the possibilities of forgiveness in the context of radical brokenness, this work makes possible the partnership of justice and transformative healing . . ." (Kristen J. Leslie, PhD, Assistant Professor of Pastoral Care and Counseling, Yale University Divinity School)*

Men's Work in Preventing Violence Against Women, edited by James Newton Poling, PhD, and Christie Cozad Neuger (Vol. 4, No. 3, 2002). *Examines the potential for men/women partnerships to work toward an end to domestic violence and sexual abuse.*

Remembering Conquest: Feminist/Womanist Perspectives on Religion, Colonization, and Sexual Violence, edited by Nantawan Boonprasat Lewis, BDiv, ThM, PhD, and Marie M. Fortune, MDiv, DHLit (Vol. 1, No. 2, 1999). *Addresses the issue of sexual violence against Native American, African American, Filipino, and Thai women from feminist/womanist theological perspectives and advocates for change in how some religious groups interpret women.*

Sexual Abuse in the Catholic Church: Trusting the Clergy?

Marie M. Fortune, MDiv, DHLit
W. Merle Longwood, PhD
Editors

Sexual Abuse in the Catholic Church: Trusting the Clergy? has been co-published simultaneously as *Journal of Religion & Abuse*, Volume 5, Number 3 2003.

The Haworth Pastoral Press®
An Imprint of The Haworth Press, Inc.

New York • London • Victoria (AU)
www.HaworthPress.com

Published by

The Haworth Pastoral Press, 10 Alice Street, Binghamton, NY 13904-1580 USA

The Haworth Pastoral Press is an imprint of The Haworth Press, Inc., 10 Alice Street, Binghamton, NY 13904-1580 USA.

Sexual Abuse in the Catholic Church: Trusting the Clergy? has been co-published simultaneously as *Journal of Religion & Abuse*, Volume 5, Number 3 2003.

© 2003 by The Haworth Press, Inc. All rights reserved. No part of this work may be reproduced or utilized in any form or by any means, electronic or mechanical, including photocopying, microfilm and recording, or by any information storage and retrieval system, without permission in writing from the publisher. Printed in the United States of America.

The development, preparation, and publication of this work has been undertaken with great care. However, the publisher, employees, editors, and agents of The Haworth Press and all imprints of The Haworth Press, Inc., including The Haworth Medical Press® and The Pharmaceutical Products Press®, are not responsible for any errors contained herein or for consequences that may ensue from use of materials or information contained in this work. Opinions expressed by the author(s) are not necessarily those of The Haworth Press, Inc.

Cover design by Marylouise E. Doyle.

Library of Congress Cataloging-in-Publication Data

Sexual abuse in the Catholic Church: trusting the clergy? / Marie M. Fortune, W. Merle Longwood, editors.
      p. cm.
     "Sexual abuse in the Catholic Church: trusting the clergy? has been co-published simultaneously as Journal of religion & abuse, volume 5, number 3 2003.
Includes bibliographical references and index.
     ISBN 0-7890-2464-0 (alk. paper) –ISBN 0-7890-2465-9 (pbk. : alk. paper)
     1. Catholic Church–Clergy–Sexual behavior–Congresses. 2. Child sexual abuse by clergy–Congresses. I. Fortune, Marie M. II. Longwood, W. Merle, 1939- III. Journal of religion & abuse
BX1912.9.S42 2004
261.8'3272'088282–dc22   2003024077

Indexing, Abstracting & Website/Internet Coverage

This section provides you with a list of major indexing & abstracting services. That is to say, each service began covering this periodical during the year noted in the right column. Most Websites which are listed below have indicated that they will either post, disseminate, compile, archive, cite or alert their own Website users with research-based content from this work. (This list is as current as the copyright date of this publication.)

(continued)

*Special Bibliographic Notes related to special journal issues
(separates) and indexing/abstracting:*

- indexing/abstracting services in this list will also cover material in any "separate" that is co-published simultaneously with Haworth's special thematic journal issue or DocuSerial. Indexing/abstracting usually covers material at the article/chapter level.
- monographic co-editions are intended for either non-subscribers or libraries which intend to purchase a second copy for their circulating collections.
- monographic co-editions are reported to all jobbers/wholesalers/approval plans. The source journal is listed as the "series" to assist the prevention of duplicate purchasing in the same manner utilized for books-in-series.
- to facilitate user/access services all indexing/abstracting services are encouraged to utilize the co-indexing entry note indicated at the bottom of the first page of each article/chapter/contribution.
- this is intended to assist a library user of any reference tool (whether print, electronic, online, or CD-ROM) to locate the monographic version if the library has purchased this version but not a subscription to the source journal.
- individual articles/chapters in any Haworth publication are also available through the Haworth Document Delivery Service (HDDS).

Sexual Abuse in the Catholic Church: Trusting the Clergy?

CONTENTS

ABOUT THE EDITORS

Marie M. Fortune, MDiv, DHLit, is The Rev. Dr. Fortune, a minister in the United Church of Christ, is the Founder of the FaithTrust Institute (formerly known as The Center for the Prevention of Sexual and Domestic Violence) in Seattle, WA, where she serves as Senior Analyst. She is the author of *Is Nothing Sacred? When Sex Invades the Pastoral Relationship; Keeping the Faith: Questions and Answers for Abused Women; Sexual Violence: The Unmentionable Sin–An Ethical and Pastoral Perspective;* and *Love Does No Harm: Sexual Ethics for the Rest of Us.* She is co-editor with Carol J. Adams of *Violence against Women and Children: A Christian Theological Sourcebook.*

W. Merle Longwood, PhD, is Professor of Religious Studies at Siena College. He teaches courses in religious thought and religious ethics. His current research interests include masculine spirituality and male sexuality and the role of religious communities in the peace process in Northern Ireland. Among his publications is *Redeeming Men: Religion and Masculinities*, which he co-edited with Stephen B. Boyd and Mark W. Muesse.

ALL HAWORTH PASTORAL PRESS
BOOKS AND JOURNALS ARE PRINTED
ON CERTIFIED ACID-FREE PAPER

About the Contributors

Ladan Alamor is Executive Director of Centro Civico of Amsterdam, Inc., a not-for-profit, community-based organization in Amsterdam, NY. Under her direction the agency provides comprehensive services to children and families of Fulton and Montgomery Counties. Centro Civico has been recognized as a model service provider, using innovative education and intervention methodologies that highlight the possibilities of transformation within Hispanic and low-income communities.

Michael J. Bland is a survivor of clergy sexual abuse, is Clinical-Pastoral Coordinator for the Office of Victim Assistance Ministry in the Catholic Archdiocese of Chicago and Clinical Counselor, Center for Psychological Services, Oak Lawn, IL. In the Chicago Archdiocese, Dr. Bland works directly with victims of sexual abuse by church personnel, including clergy. He was a member of the panel that addressed the Dallas meeting on clergy sexual abuse of the U.S. Conference of Catholic Bishops in a "Session for the Media by Experts." He is also a member of the National Review Board for the U.S. Conference of Catholic Bishops.

The Rev. Donald B. Cozzens is Professor of Religious Studies at John Carroll University in Cleveland. He was previously President-Rector and Professor of Pastoral Theology at Saint Mary Seminary and Graduate School of Theology in Cleveland. Among his publications are *The Spirituality of the Diocesan Priest*, which he edited, and two recent books, *The Changing Face of the Priesthood: A Reflection on the Priest's Crisis of Soul* and *Sacred Silence: Denial and the Crisis in the Church* (which is reviewed in this issue).

James S. Dalton is Professor and Chair of the Department of Religious Studies at Siena College. He teaches courses in the history of religions and the history of western religions. His research has combined history of Christianity and history of religions. His current research is focused on the "religious imagination" and on contact studies involving the mutual image creation of Native Americans and European Americans.

The Rev. James S. Evinger coordinates clinical research, University of Rochester Medical Center, Rochester, NY, and is a chaplain, New York State Office of Mental Retardation and Developmental Disabilities.

The Most Rev. Harry J. Flynn is Archbishop of the Archdiocese of Saint Paul and Minneapolis. He previously was the Bishop of the Diocese of Lafayette, LA until being named Coadjutor Archbishop for the Archdiocese of Saint Paul and Minneapolis. He is a member of the United States Catholic Conference of Bishops (USCCB) Committee on African American Catholics. As Chair of the USCCB Ad Hoc Committee on Sexual Abuse, he played a key role in the development of the guidelines for responding to clergy sexual abuse approved at the USCCB meetings in Dallas and Washington, DC in 2002.

Mary E. Hunt is a Catholic feminist theologian. She is the co-founder and co-director of the Women's Alliance for Theology, Ethics, and Ritual (WATER) in Silver Spring, Maryland.

The Most Rev. Howard J. Hubbard is Bishop of the Catholic Diocese of Albany. He has served as a delegate to the White House Conference on Families, Chair of the Bishops' Committee on Human Values, Marriage, and the Family, and member of the Catholic Campaign for Human Development, Social Policy, and World Peace. He was appointed by Pope John Paul II to be a member of the Secretariat for Non-Believers. He is a member of the United States Conference of Catholic Bishops' Ad Hoc Committee on Sexual Abuse.

The Rev. Karen Lebacqz is the Robert Gordon Sproul Professor of Theological Ethics at Pacific School of Religion in Berkeley, California. An ordained minister in the United Church of Christ, she has taught and lectured on sexual ethics and professional ethics for 30 years.

W. Merle Longwood is Professor or Religious Studies at Siena College. He teaches courses in religious thought and religious ethics. His current research interests include masculine spirituality and male sexuality and the role of religious communities in the peace process in Northern Ireland. Among his publications is *Redeeming Men: Religious and Masculinities*, which he co-edited with Stephen B. Boyd and Mark W. Muesse.

The Rev. Kevin E. Mackin is President and Professor of Religious Studies at Siena College. As a priest of the Order of Friars Minor, he has held a number of positions in the Province of the Most Holy Name of Jesus. His teaching and research have focused particularly on ecumenical Christianity, and his writings include *In Search of the Authentic Christian Tradition*. He has served on various national, diocesan, Franciscan, and educational committees. He is currently Vice Chair of the Association of Franciscan Colleges and Universities.

Robert L. Miller, Jr. is Assistant Professor of Social Welfare and member of the Institute of Minority Health for the School of Public Health at the State University of New York at Albany. His current research integrates social welfare, public health and spirituality, with a particular focus on how African Americans living with HIV disease use spirituality as a coping strategy. He is the author of *African American Churches at the Crossroads of AIDS and Spirituality* and *Professional Social Work: Implications for Practice, Research, and Education.*

Carolyn Moore Newberger is Assistant Clinical Professor of Psychology, Department of Psychiatry, Harvard Medical School and Associate in Psychology, Children's Hospital/Judge Baker Children's Center, Boston. She has had extensive national and international involvement in research and education related to child abuse. Her research interests include child sexual abuse and its consequences and family violence and development across the life-span. She has received numerous awards and has written numerous articles in professional journals about the effects of sexual abuse on children.

Anne M. Pope is President of the Albany Branch of the NAACP; Director of the New York African American Research Foundation; and Vice Chair of the Advisory Board of the Martin Luther King, Jr. and Coretta Scott King Lecture Series on Race and Nonviolent Social Change at Siena College. She has been active in many efforts that seek to obtain social justice for people of color and other disadvantaged people and is a long-time active member of Union Missionary Baptist Church in Albany, NY.

Foreword

The churches, Catholic and non-Catholic alike, have been reeling from increasing numbers of reports of the sexual abuse of children and adolescents by clergy both in the United States and beyond (Ireland, the United Kingdom, Continental Europe, Australia). Reports of such abuse date back to the 1980s and became public and controversial in the early 1990s. The issues expanded beyond sexual abuse and its consequences for the victims. Now the credibility of the churches themselves came into question with accusations of "cover ups" by those in authority in the churches. The role of the bishops in the Catholic Church served to focus the issue as one of institutional structure and responsibility as well as one of pastoral care. The tragic and shattered lives of victims raised questions about whether or not the clergy could be trusted to care for the most helpless and vulnerable among us. What was to be done to begin to heal the lives of the victims and restore trust in the institutions from which the perpetrators came? These were the circumstances and issues that brought together 415 Catholics and non-Catholics, clergy, laity, and victims of sexual abuse at Siena College on Saturday, March 29, 2003. This volume represents the conclusions and insights of this day and is presented as one moment in the process of healing and rebuilding trust between religious communities and those who are served by these communities.

What role can a college such as Siena and the scholars and practitioners who assembled on a Saturday in late March play in this process of healing and trust building? The role of an academic institution such as Siena, and its Religious Studies Department, is to enable a moment of reflection in the larger movement toward healing and trust. This mo-

[Haworth co-indexing entry note]: "Foreword." Dalton, Jim. Co-published simultaneously in *Journal of Religion & Abuse* (The Haworth Pastoral Press, an imprint of The Haworth Press, Inc.) Vol. 5, No. 3, 2003, pp. xvii-xx; and: *Sexual Abuse in the Catholic Church: Trusting the Clergy?* (ed: Marie M. Fortune, and W. Merle Longwood) The Haworth Pastoral Press, an imprint of The Haworth Press, Inc., 2003, pp. xv-xviii. Single or multiple copies of this article are available for a fee from The Haworth Document Delivery Service [1-800-HAWORTH, 9:00 a.m. - 5:00 p.m. (EST). E-mail address: docdelivery@haworthpress.com].

© 2003 by The Haworth Press, Inc. All rights reserved.

ment of reflection is not the whole story. Rather, it is the portion of the story where questions can be raised and answers provisionally offered. How have we come to where we are? What must we do to move on? The symposium, its distinguished scholars, clergy, and community leaders and this volume resulting from that gathering, was and is meant to reflect, raise questions, and provide potential new directions during a painful moment in the lives of the churches.

The Department of Religious Studies at Siena College sees, as one aspect of its mission, a responsibility to bring such academic reflection to the major questions that engage the churches as well as the public at the beginning of the twenty-first century. The sexual abuse of children and adolescents by clergy, especially made visible in the American Roman Catholic Church, has become a topic of intense debate and extensive publicity over the last two years and, alas, over the last two decades. The events at Dallas, Texas, where the American Catholic bishops assembled in June of 2002 and the subsequent suspension of priests in our own Roman Catholic Diocese of Albany with extensive media coverage brought the Religious Studies faculty to ask what our contribution might be to the ongoing dialogue and debate. Could we shed light on an issue that had become so superheated by the attention of the media and the justified anger of the victims? Might it now be possible to step back and provide reasoned analysis to such a painful topic? Our answer was "yes" and the Symposium and the present study are the result.

Although we initially planned a modest local gathering of Siena faculty and students, this soon grew to a nationally focused Symposium with the encouragement and support of Fr. Kevin Mackin, OFM, President of Siena College. Dr. Merle Longwood and I agreed to co-chair this effort and to bring to Siena an ecumenical and interdisciplinary group of scholars, both regionally and nationally known, to address the question "Trusting the Clergy? The Churches and Communities Come to Grips with Sexual Misconduct." Co-sponsoring this event, along with the Religious Studies Department, were the Department of Social Work and the Office of the Chaplain at Siena, the Roman Catholic Diocese of Albany, the Capital Area Council of Churches, and the Capital Region Ecumenical Organization.

Our efforts commenced with the organization of a Planning Committee consisting of representatives of Siena's Religious Studies Department (myself and Dr. Longwood), the Social Work Department (Professor Diane Strock-Lynskey), the Chaplain of the College (Fr. William Beaudin, OFM), the Chancellor of the Roman Catholic Diocese of Albany (Fr.

Kenneth Doyle), the former Executive Director of the Capital Area Council of Churches (Rev. Dr. Robert C. Lamar), and the President of the Capital Region Ecumenical Organization (Rev. Donna Elia). The composition of this Committee was intended to signal that we saw the crisis as not just a Roman Catholic issue, but as one that crossed denominational lines. This Planning Committee worked assiduously over a period of eight months to lay out the parameters of the questions, define the two major foci of the day including the morning ("The Sexual Abuse Crisis: What Have We Learned?") and the afternoon ("The Sexual Abuse Crisis: What Issues Do We Still Have to Face?"), and develop a list of participants.

In addition to the distinguished clergy (Archbishop Harry J. Flynn and Bishop Howard J. Hubbard) and national scholars (Rev. Dr. Donald B. Cozzens, Rev. Dr. Marie M. Fortune, Dr. Michael J. Bland, Dr. Carolyn M. Newberger), the Planning Committee included voices from regional multicultural communities in the persons of Ms. Ladan Alomar (the Director of Centro Civico in Amsterdam, New York), Dr. Robert L. Miller, Jr., CSW (a faculty member in the Social Work Department at the State University at Albany and an expert on issues relating to the African American gay community and AIDS) and Ms. Anne Pope (President of the Albany Branch of the NAACP and a member of Union Missionary Baptist Church in Albany, New York). Our question to these latter communities was how the crisis in the Catholic Church and beyond affected the Hispanic, African American, and gay and lesbian communities. What now was the status of religious institutions among them? The high quality of the presentations and their enthusiastic reception by the audience fully justified the judgments of the Planning Committee in its invitations both national and regional.

The Symposium was publicized nationally through media organs such as *The National Catholic Reporter, America, The Christian Century, The Council on Social Work Education Reporter, The National Association of Social Workers National Newsletter* and *The Chronicle of Higher Education.* An article appeared early in *The Daily Gazette,* one of the major regional newspapers. Portions of this article were picked up by the Associated Press and appeared in various newspapers throughout the country. Press representatives were present at the Symposium and reported aspects of the events of the day. The Albany Diocesan newspaper, *The Evangelist,* did an extensive six-page series of articles covering the Symposium. In addition, responses to the day in the form of letters, emails, and phone conversations were uniformly positive. Many requested the papers of the Symposium. Proceeding to publication, strongly contemplated from the beginning, was now certain. Clearly the Symposium had touched on the issues and provided some important reflections on the ongoing crisis. However, it must be pointed out that this publication is only one beginning in a conversation involving victims, perpetrators, institutions, and scholars that must continue. It is to be hoped that this contribution will encourage others, both within and outside of academe, to move the dialogue further along the road to healing and trust.

A volume such as this is not possible without the work and cooperation of many hands. My thanks must go first and foremost to my co-chair (and the co-editor of this work), Dr. Merle Longwood. Thanks must also be given to the Planning Committee mentioned above, the President of Siena College, the speakers at the Symposium and contributors to this volume, especially to the Reverend Dr. Marie Fortune who both presented at the Symposium and co-edited the publication of this volume coming out of it. In addition, the generous work of all of those who made the Symposium possible, in various supporting roles, such as Ms. Lynn McGarry, secretary *extraordinaire*, and Mr. Bill Dallas and his events crew who gave both the audience and the participants such a fulfilling and meaningful experience. Often those go unnoticed, from food service providers to bookstore salespersons, who make such an event possible for those who headline and attend. Finally, we must thank the audience that attended the Symposium on March 29 for its perceptive questions, heartfelt dialogue, and careful attention. The passage from the original presentations to the final published remarks owes very much to this attentive and perceptive audience.

James S. Dalton

Introduction

W. Merle Longwood

The issue of clergy sexual abuse burst onto the scene of American Catholicism during the decade of the 1980s, and Peter Steinfels, in an article, "The Church's Sex-Abuse Crisis," in *Commonweal Magazine*, emphasizes that the pivotal years were 1985-1993, when "the American bishops were dragged kicking and screaming into dealing with the sexual abuse by priests" (Steinfels, 2002).

This collection of essays makes a contribution to understanding the ways in which the American Catholic bishops have dealt, or are attempting to deal with, the scandal that has increasingly occupied the attention of the American media since the mid-1980s, with its pinnacle year being 2002, when the investigative reporting by the staff of *The Boston Globe* told the story about scores of abusive priests who molested children and the senior officials in the Catholic Church who covered up their crimes (*Boston Globe*, 2002), eventually bringing about the resignation of Cardinal Bernard Law.

Because there is no systematic historical documentation, it is not possible to know whether sexual abuse by clergy has been a relatively constant problem going back centuries (Sipe, 1995) or a recent phenomenon, perhaps beginning in the 1960s with a genuine increase in abusive behavior occurring as a result of relaxed discipline and changed cultural standards (Jenkins, 1996). Likewise, we do not know how sexual abuse in the Catholic Church is similar to or different from what happens in other Christian churches, because there is no organization that keeps rec-

[Haworth co-indexing entry note]: "Introduction." Longwood, W. Merle. Co-published simultaneously in *Journal of Religion & Abuse* (The Haworth Pastoral Press, an imprint of The Haworth Press, Inc.) Vol. 5, No. 3, 2003, pp. 1-7; and: *Sexual Abuse in the Catholic Church: Trusting the Clergy?* (ed: Marie M. Fortune, and W. Merle Longwood) The Haworth Pastoral Press, an imprint of The Haworth Press, Inc., 2003, pp. 1-7. Single or multiple copies of this article are available for a fee from The Haworth Document Delivery Service [1-800-HAWORTH, 9:00 a.m. - 5:00 p.m. (EST). E-mail address: docdelivery@haworthpress.com].

http://www.haworthpress.com/web/JORA
© 2003 by The Haworth Press, Inc. All rights reserved.
Digital Object Identifier: 10.1300/J154v05n03_01

ords of abusive clergy in all the denominations, though we know there have been allegations in recent years of clergy molestation against Episcopal, Lutheran, Presbyterian, Methodist, Baptist, United Church of Christ, Greek Orthodox, and other non-Catholic clergy. In addition, we do not know how the nature and incidence of clergy sexual abuse of minors in the United States differs from other countries; we do know that there have been reports, recent and old, of such abuse among Catholic clergy in Canada, Ireland, Britain, Australia, France, Austria, and Poland.

With an awareness that this was not a phenomenon unique to the United States and a belief that it is not totally unique to our time in history, a group of us at Siena College in collaboration with leaders of the ecumenical Christian community in the Capital Region of New York acknowledged that the media had provided a service to the church in exposing what had been shrouded in darkness, but we were convinced that there was need for a more careful analysis from a variety of perspectives of the deeper roots that had led to this crisis. As we set out to plan a symposium for the academic, ecumenical religious and wider communities, we were pleased that the people whom we asked to come to speak at this day-long forum, many with international reputations, immediately said they would be pleased to participate.

The format of our symposium included morning and afternoon keynote addresses, each of which was responded to by a diverse panel, creating a dialogue among experts; an additional panel representing "Voices from Multicultural Communities"; and a closing panel in which all the symposium presenters responded to audience questions. All of the presentations except for the informal responses given in the wrap-up panel are included in this collection of essays.

The first keynote was given by Archbishop Harry J. Flynn, who provided a bishop's perspective on the sexual abuse crisis, beginning with his experience in the diocese of Lafayette, Louisiana, when as newly appointed bishop in the late 1980s he confronted the difficult issues that emerged from a case of clergy sexual misconduct in that diocese. The effectiveness of his pastoral and administrative response to this situation brought him national attention, so it was not surprising that he was named to the United States Catholic Conference of Bishops (USCCB) Ad Hoc Committee on Sexual Abuse that was formed in 1993. When the Committee was reconstituted to include representatives of each of the fourteen episcopal regions of the American Catholic Church in 2002, he was asked to serve as its chair.

Much of Flynn's essay describes how the Bishops' Conference over time developed principles and procedures to respond to the issues of clergy sexual abuse, beginning in the late 1980s with the formulation of five principles and culminating in 2002 with the adoption of the *Charter for the Protection of Children and Young People*. Implementation of the *Charter* included the establishment of a National Review Board and an Office for Child and Youth Protection. Former Oklahoma Governor Frank Keating was named as Chair of the National Review Board, but he resigned after one year after having made public his dismay at the lack of cooperation the Board had experienced from some of the nation's bishops (NCCBUSCC, 2003)). Ms. Kathleen McChesney was appointed to be director of the Office for Child and Youth Protection.

Archbishop Flynn emphasizes that, contrary to popular opinion, the USCCB "is not a governing body. It is an association of bishops intended to explore more unified pastoral responses to issues of common concern, but its deliberative power to make decisions binding on all bishops is very limited." Michael Bland, one of the charter members of the National Review Board who had himself been a victim of clergy sexual abuse, in his response to Archbishop Flynn gives a different perspective on this. He argues that the *Charter for the Protection of Children and Young People* is binding "all the bishops of the United States to a uniform code of action and response in the event of accusations and instances of sexual abuse." Flynn is presumably acknowledging that according to canon law, the powers of the bishops' Conference are almost entirely advisory, so that the Conference can cajole and coax but never demand adherence to anything resembling a national policy. Though Flynn states that what had been put in place by the Conference, and approved by the Vatican, is "a set of national standards," he goes on to say that, "we do not see this as an imposition on the dioceses but as a way for each diocese to monitor its own response and to enable all dioceses to be accountable to one another." An important question, then, is what power, beyond moral suasion, the *Charter* and its implementation through the National Review Board and the Office for Child and Youth Protection has to bring about cooperation on the part of individual bishops?

That question relates to the major critique that Marie Fortune, in her response to Archbishop Flynn, makes of the Catholic bishops' actions. Distinguishing "an institutional protection agenda" from "a justice-making agenda," Fortune observes, "These longstanding cases of abuses by priests, silence, and cover up are all the evidence we need that the hierarchy has been hijacked by those who chose the institutional protection agenda," which she believes "is still holding sway in most dioceses." She claims that the justice-making agenda is one that believes "that God calls us to stand with those who are most vulnerable, that making justice and healing are holy works, and that the church has the theological and spiritual resources actually to respond to this crisis."

Carolyn Moore Newberger, in her response to Archbishop Flynn, did not really challenge what he had said but suggested an important perspective that needed to be added to it. She commented, "In his presentation, Archbishop Harry J. Flynn talked about looking through the eyes of the victims and the parents. . . . I would also argue that it is important to look through the eyes of abusers." She elaborates some effects that sexual abuse has when viewed through "the eyes of victims" and the implications of this for how these victims should be treated very respectfully. But the main thrust of her response is to describe the modes of operation and motivations that drive child sexual abusers, the majority of whom are male. She cautions, "As a consequence, you have to assume that people who want access to children–people who seek opportunity, secrecy, and power and credibility with children to groom them for sexual relationships–will enter the priesthood."

In the second keynote, Fr. Donald B. Cozzens summarizes what we have learned from the clergy abuse crisis, and then moves to the systemic issues that need to be examined–not just personal relationships but issues of structure and meaning. He echoes Fortune in acknowledging that leaders in the churches have too often acted like attorneys rather than shepherds, protecting the interests of the church and its priests, rather than attending to the welfare of those who have been wounded by clergy abuse. He calls for transparency and accountability, suggesting there is need for empirical studies to determine the number of priests who have been involved in abusive behavior in comparison to the total number of priests and clergy of other denominations, and he calls upon the institutional church to acknowledge openly the actual costs that have been incurred as a result of clergy misconduct. He suggests, but does not fully develop, the idea of accountability that is not just upward in the ecclesial hierarchy but outward to include the broader community, suggesting intriguingly a new role for parents. Throughout his essay, he emphasizes that the issues to be addressed are not just about individual behaviors, but about systemic, structural issues, including issues about ecclesial structure and the culture of priesthood.

In her response to Cozzens, Fortune continues to spell out the implications of what the church would be like if it were to pursue a justice-making agenda and not an institutional-protection agenda. She broadens the base in the discussion of sexual abuse by suggesting that the important question "moves beyond the immediate crisis of disclosures of sexual abuse of children and includes sexual abuse of adults also. The issue is not even about sex per se but about exploitation of vulnerability, regardless of the age of the victim. Slowly the reality of adult women and some men whose pastoral relationships have been violated by priests are coming to the fore. This will be the next wave of the tsunami to hit the church." Those who have been observing the issue of sexual abuse in a broader framework, including the planners of this symposium, would agree that that these are issues that have come to the fore in the Catholic Church in other cultures, such as Africa, as well as in Protestant and Orthodox denominations worldwide, but those at this symposium were not ready to pick up on this broader agenda.

Fortune spells out in detail why it is wrong for a member of the clergy to have sexual activity with someone whom he/she serves or supervises, but then she takes the Catholic bishops to task by saying that in their discussion of the abuse of children in the *Dallas Charter* they "got the wrong commandment." Instead of the 6th commandment, forbidding adultery, "they should have gone to the 7th, 'You shall not steal.' . . . To sexually abuse a child is to steal their innocence and their future, often with profound and tragic consequences."

Bishop Howard Hubbard agrees with much of what Fr. Cozzens presented, acknowledging that many bishops had given greater priority to protecting the church than to the protection of children, and he welcomes the call for the laity to take a greater role in the leadership of the church. He concurs with Fr. Cozzens' call for transparency and accountability about "the number of perpetrators, victims, and costs associated with the scandal." And he seems to go beyond Archbishop Flynn's cautious view about the role the USCCB can play in relation to individual bishops when he states that he believed the National Review Board, then chaired by former Governor Keating, could make a significant difference in getting those figures, "and any diocesan bishop who does not comply should be subject to censure or removal."

Hubbard stresses that he believed the National Review Board could make a significant contribution to accountability by commissioning research on the data it compiles, and he points to the study of the John Jay College of Criminal Justice that had already been commissioned by the Board. What he does not say is that there was initial resistance to participation in this study by a number of bishops, though the John Jay research team indicates it is now receiving greater cooperation and believes that its final study will reflect the vast majority of dioceses/eparchies since 1950, though not all (USCCB, National Review Board, 2003). Again this illustrates the difficulty of establishing by voluntary consent, in the absence of canon law, a national policy to which dioceses can be held publicly accountable.

But Hubbard focuses most of his comments on the complexities in "translating into reality the vision that Fr. Cozzens has articulated." He refers to the complexity of legal responsibility and how to disentangle that from moral responsibility. He particularly challenges Cozzens' statement that "we must put the spiritual and personal welfare of those wounded ahead of everything else, including the welfare of our respective institutions," suggesting that alternatively there has to be a concern for balancing this "good" in relation to all the other "goods" that the church offers to its members and to the wider society in terms of spiritual, academic, health care, and social programs. Finally, he proposes a model of restorative justice as the foundation for bringing about healing and reconciliation between victims of abuse and church leaders, rather than the adversarial system that now prevails.

Carolyn Newberger does not directly respond to Fr. Cozzens but takes up on her own the theme of his essay and proposed her own suggestions for issues concerning sexual abuse in the Catholic Church that still have to be faced: "How do we know what the truth is when there are sexual abuse allegations; and how do we protect children from such abuse?" She referred to specific articles in the *Charter for the Protection of Children and Young People* that Archbishop Flynn had addressed, pointing out the complexities in interpreting and implementing them. She illustrates the problem of interpreting the phrase "reason to believe" by asking how you determine who to believe when there are conflicting stories, the alleged victim's and the alleged perpetrator's.

Newberger describes how difficult it is to understand how children disclose sexual abuse, which they often do indirectly and often fail to disclose at all for fear and/or respect they have in relation to the abuser. She suggests that unless people understand the ways children disclose, they are likely to dismiss the disclosures as not believable. She proposes some basic questions to help sort out the truth, such as: "Why would a child lie to get into trouble?" Or in an ambiguous situation, one can ask the question: "Who has the greatest motive to lie?" Realizing that there are consequences involved in making an error in judgment, she suggested that the more tolerable error is to believe the child, even if it means that an innocent priest may suffer emotionally and professionally rather than to believe a priest with the risk that that child or other children may continue to be molested.

She concludes by bringing up the issue of divorce, suggesting that the Dallas Charter recognizes that some predatory priests must be "divorced" from the clerical state, and she poses the question whether a woman who might be married to a predatory husband who endangers her or their children should not likewise be supported by the church in ending her marriage.

The "Voices from Multicultural Communities" Panel included Ladan Alomar, Anne M. Pope, and Dr. Robert L. Miller, Jr, CSW. Ladan Alomar and Anne Pope, in particular, draw upon their experiences in the Latina and African American communities to discuss how the clergy sexual abuse crisis in the Catholic Church has had an impact upon them. Robert Miller, after acknowledging how many people have been harmed by homophobia in the church, proposed that people who had been wounded by clergy sexual abuse use spirituality to reframe their relationship with the church as they redefined the church.

The success of this collection of essays is dependent upon how well it engages you, not just to accept what someone else has said but to engage yourself in the dialogue. This will encourage people to seek together to listen to and tell the truth in love for the sake of healing and restoring justice for all people.

REFERENCES

Boston Globe Investigative Staff. (2002) *Betrayal: The Crisis in the Catholic Church.* Boston: Little, Brown, and Co.

Jenkins, Philip. (1996) *Pedophiles and Priests: Anatomy of a Contemporary Crisis.* New York: Oxford University Press, pp. 33-34.

NCCBUSCC. (2003) *www.nccbuscc.org/comm/archives/2003/03-128.htm.*

Sipe, A.W. Richard. (1995) *Sex, Priests, and Power: Anatomy of a Crisis.* New York: Brunner/Mazel, Inc., pp. 10-12.

Steinfels, Peter. (2002) "The Church's Sex-Abuse Crisis," *Commonweal Magazine* (www.commonwealmagazine.org/2002april192002/41902ar.htm).

USCCB. (2003) *Report of the National Review Board,* Chicago, July 29, 2003 *www.jusccbb.org/comm/reviewboard.htm.*

Symposium Greetings

Kevin E. Mackin

SUMMARY. Fr. Mackin, President of Siena College, which hosted the symposium on "Trusting the Clergy?" welcomed the audience and set the tone for the day (March 29, 2003). *[Article copies available for a fee from The Haworth Document Delivery Service: 1-800-HAWORTH. E-mail address: <docdelivery@haworthpress.com> Website:<http://www.HaworthPress.com> © 2003 by The Haworth Press, Inc. All rights reserved.]*

KEYWORDS. Sexual abuse by clergy, Roman Catholic sex abuse crisis

To the twenty-four wars being waged in our world, another was added last week, in Iraq. While we have more access than ever to coverage, more images of missiles and explosions and injuries, there is often more heat than light.

This symposium on coming to grips with sexual misconduct by priests is crucial in order to shed light on the national problem of sexual abuse by clergy. Abuse afflicts society, in many sectors. Why, then, if a member of the clergy is accused, does it seem to be reported so widely? I suspect it is because society expects better of the Church. Society expects us to be leaders, to behave with integrity, to be trustworthy.

Some data suggest that fewer than 2% of priests have engaged in sexual abuse. Comparative evidence indicates that most priests are reasonably mature and happy.

[Haworth co-indexing entry note]: "Symposium Greetings." Mackin, Kevin E. Co-published simultaneously in *Journal of Religion & Abuse* (The Haworth Pastoral Press, an imprint of The Haworth Press, Inc.) Vol. 5, No. 3, 2003, pp. 9-11; and: *Sexual Abuse in the Catholic Church: Trusting the Clergy?* (ed: Marie M. Fortune, and W. Merle Longwood) The Haworth Pastoral Press, an imprint of The Haworth Press, Inc., 2003, pp. 9-11. Single or multiple copies of this article are available for a fee from The Haworth Document Delivery Service [1-800-HAWORTH, 9:00 a.m. - 5:00 p.m. (EST). E-mail address: docdelivery@haworthpress.com].

http://www.haworthpress.com/web/JORA
© 2003 by The Haworth Press, Inc. All rights reserved.
Digital Object Identifier: 10.1300/J154v05n03_02

A clergy peccadillo, because it's rare and if it's alleged in public with a demand for public penance, seems to reach a news level of "If it bleeds, it leads." This is not to say that reports of misconduct are always accurate.

Nearly two centuries ago, "The Awful Disclosures of Maria Monk," purportedly written by a former nun, described a convent as "a harem of the local priesthood." I dare say that is not the experience of the convents we know where women religious do their best to live out Gospel values in community. In fact, an anti-Catholic organization instigated the Maria Monk publication. Eventually, Protestants and Catholics studied the facts, found "The Awful Disclosures" faulty, and published a refutation.

But by no means should we blame anti-Catholic tactics, while ignoring what some members of our communities may have actually done, and the needs of their victims. One of the failures in our church communities has been the issue of accountability. The viability of our mission–to proclaim the Gospel together–depends on mutual trust.

Today's academic program, involving clergy and lay presenters from various church communities, is a hopeful sign, because it indicates we are willing to learn together, to work better together in our common mission. Above all, the Gospels teach us that a Christian community is one in which it can be known, as scripture says, "See how they love one another." The good works of our church communities are clear in the areas of feeding the hungry and speaking out for the powerless. Our hospitals have been at the forefront of caring for the uninsured, for persons with AIDS, and for other vulnerable people. Our schools are institutions of hope for children who might otherwise be relegated to mean streets. In short, we have been recognized for helping "the least of our brothers and sisters."

Our church-based social service systems have contributed much to the achievements of our nation. All of this has been supported, in large part, by faithful laypersons. Their faith in what clergy preach–faith in the Good News–is inspiring. If the news has not been very good for the past couple of years, I submit we need to develop a new paradigm.

I am not saying we should copy a paradigm of corporate lingo and strategies. On the contrary, Christians are expected to be countersigns, and clergy and church leaders to be trustworthy above all, as disciplined confidants and instruments of peace. This is a good thing. Certainly, we are taking steps to do this in accountability to mission, and the continued renewal of our partnership with lay leaders, a tradition that goes back some 2000 years.

Jesus Christ's paradigm was to call forth the gifts of people and to wash their feet. Calling forth our gifts means taking a closer look at what our gifts and services are. Embracing Christ's paradigm in modern times includes being countersigns to violence in society, to a lack of business ethics, and to sexual misbehaviors that objectify and demean persons. Sexual abuse in society appears to have increased in the post war years of the 20th century. Just a couple of statistics: The incidence of sexual abuse in America has been estimated at one in three females, and one in five males (Finkelhorn, 1986). Assuming that this national study holds on average, some 60 million Americans have been sexually abused. We can surmise most of that is not by priests or ministers. But religious communities, while taking the heat, can help shed light on this problem. It's about time we came to grips with it.

Siena College encourages learning, through academic inquiry and the exchange and critique of related ideas. You might say we test information through a lens of scholarly process. Moreover, in a Franciscan Catholic academic community such as ours, with faith in a provident God, we can be an agent of positive change. Today's academic program will shed light on aspects of abuse, trust, and faith, so that we may better address the needs of society.

REFERENCE

Finkelhorn, David (1986). *A Source Book on Child Sexual Abuse: New Theory and Research*. Beverly Hills: Sage Publications.

Keynote:
Dallas and Beyond–
Perspectives of a Bishop and Pastor

Harry J. Flynn

SUMMARY. Archbishop Flynn's keynote at the "Trusting the Clergy?" Symposium is a bishop's perspective on the work of the United States Catholic Bishops' Conference at its Dallas meeting (2002) and for the future to overcome the problem of sexual abuse of children and young people by clergy and to heal the wounds this sinful and criminal behavior has inflicted on the church in the U.S. *[Article copies available for a fee from The Haworth Document Delivery Service: 1-800-HAWORTH. E-mail address: <docdelivery@haworthpress.com> Website: <http://www. HaworthPress.com> © 2003 by The Haworth Press, Inc. All rights reserved.]*

KEYWORDS. Archbishop Harry J. Flynn, clergy sexual abuse, Roman Catholic sex abuse crisis

As a guest here in Albany, I want to take the opportunity to compliment your own bishop, Howard Hubbard, for his leadership in this area. Bishop Hubbard, as you know, offered an amendment in Dallas sug-

[Haworth co-indexing entry note]: "Keynote: Dallas and Beyond–Perspectives of a Bishop and Pastor." Flynn, Harry J. Co-published simultaneously in *Journal of Religion & Abuse* (The Haworth Pastoral Press, an imprint of The Haworth Press, Inc.) Vol. 5, No. 3, 2003, pp. 13-21; and: *Sexual Abuse in the Catholic Church: Trusting the Clergy?* (ed: Marie M. Fortune, and W. Merle Longwood) The Haworth Pastoral Press, an imprint of The Haworth Press, Inc., 2003, pp. 13-21. Single or multiple copies of this article are available for a fee from The Haworth Document Delivery Service [1-800-HAWORTH. 9:00 a.m. - 5:00 p.m. (EST). E-mail address: docdelivery@haworthpress.com].

http://www.haworthpress.com/web/JORA
© 2003 by The Haworth Press, Inc. All rights reserved.
Digital Object Identifier: 10.1300/J154v05n03_03

13

gesting a case-by-case evaluation of offenses occurring many years ago. But when that amendment was defeated, Bishop Hubbard set aside his personal views and voted in favor of the zero-tolerance policy and went right home and implemented it, removing six priests within two weeks. He has also been a leader, for many years, in offering compassionate support for victims and last month at the urging of Bishop Hubbard, 500 church staff members were trained in prevention of child sexual abuse. I really think you have right here locally a bishop who is a model brother of spiritual and pastoral leadership during one of the most difficult times in the history of the American Catholic Church.

My experience of this problem as a bishop goes back to the place and almost to the time of the first case of this kind to gain widespread public attention. This was in the Diocese of Lafayette, Louisiana. I was appointed coadjutor bishop there in 1986, and I became diocesan bishop in 1989. I served there until 1994 when I was appointed Coadjutor Archbishop of Saint Paul and Minneapolis.

The faith life of the Catholics of the Lafayette diocese, in the past, could be described as devout and uncomplicated; but it had become terribly complicated by the abuse committed by one priest in particular and the criticism of how the matter had been handled by the diocese. One of the things that gives me hope in the current crisis is the experience I had in Lafayette of how people of good faith dealt with these terrible happenings. They were able, in a period of great testing, ultimately to discern between the grievous failings of the church's ministers and the truth and integrity of her Gospel message.

This is not a mere wishful thinking. The local church of Lafayette came to this realization only after suffering a great deal in facing up to the terrible things done to innocent children by men who should be among the most trustworthy in the community. For a while it was not easy being a Catholic–and definitely not a priest or a bishop–in Lafayette. I realize also that some people have never healed from this wound; but I can say that the diocese overall did experience the truth of what St. Paul wrote and our Holy Father referred to last April in his address to the U.S. cardinals and officers during the meeting with the prefects of several Roman congregations ("Final Communiqué of Vatican-U.S. Church Leaders Summit," *Origins*, pp. 771-77): "where sin increased, grace overflowed all the more" (cf. Rom 5:20).

The events in Lafayette inspired the first discussion among the U.S. Catholic bishops of this problem on the national level. Throughout the late 1980s dioceses began developing policies. In 1992, the terrible case of James Porter, who was a serial abuser in three states, alerted the bishops that more needed to be done at the national level. The bishops realized they needed to:

- respond promptly to all allegations of abuse where there is reasonable belief that abuse has occurred;
- if an allegation is supported by sufficient evidence, relieve the alleged offender promptly of his ministerial duties and refer him for appropriate medical evaluation and intervention;
- comply with the obligations of civil law as regards reporting of the incident and cooperating with the investigation;
- reach out to the victims and their families and communicate sincere commitment to their spiritual and emotional well-being;
- deal as openly as possible with the members of the community, within the confines of respect for privacy of the individuals involved.

These five principles became the core of the developing diocesan policies and would also be the starting point for the Charter for the Protection of Children and Young People (U.S.C.C.B, "Charter for the Protection of Children and Young People Revised Edition, 2002."). In February, 1993, the Bishops' Committee on Priestly Life and Ministry sponsored a "think tank" in St. Louis which drew experts on the issue and concerned parties from around the nation. I participated in that "think tank." It was an enlightening experience that touched the emotions of the participants as well as our minds. It made many recommendations which were very helpful when the Conference established the Ad Hoc Committee on Sexual Abuse in June, 1993 to provide a more regular monitoring of the problem.

This Committee reviewed the existing diocesan policies, made recommendations for improving them, led discussions of the various aspects of the problem at the bishops' meetings, met with victims or attended meetings of their groups, and engaged in international meetings of hierarchies facing the same problems.

There was a substantial decline in the number of new cases throughout the later 1990s. One indication of this is that some treatment centers that concentrated their attention on perpetrators of clergy sexual abuse had to begin to emphasize other psychological problems if they were going to maintain a sufficient client base.

The media on the national level, which had followed the problem avidly in the first half of the 1990s, ceased to pay much attention to it after 1996.

Although current critics still raise the specter of bishops shuffling priests from parish to parish, this is not an accurate or fair characterization of the bishops' actions in the last decade. Whatever may have been the facts years ago–and it is important to recall that not only the church but society in general, including law enforcement officials and psychologists, has learned a lot more about this problem than was known even 20 years ago–in the last decade, bishops have approached such priests with an awareness that some have psycho-sexual maladies that can be controlled but never cured. No bishop thinks today–nor have they thought for many years now–that a change of assignment could adequately address their illness.

In 1993, I was asked to serve on the Conference's first Ad Hoc Committee on Sexual Abuse. As we did our work, we believed that we shared with the public, whether Catholic or non-Catholic, information about the important work that Committee did. Certainly Bishop John Kinney deserved the thanks of his brother bishops for untiringly speaking to this issue in the media for the bishops' conference in those earlier years of crisis.

The media–which paid the Ad Hoc Committee such close attention in those days–this year seemed to have forgotten about its work. In publicizing cases going back several and even many years–cases those same media outlets had often already covered themselves–a largely distorted impression was created in the mind of the general public about how seriously the bishops individually and as a national body had already confronted the problem.

In the last decade–and before–bishops have met with victims, removed priests, and made the required reports to civil authorities. Was every case handled as well as it could have been and was every diocese at the same level of response? Clearly not. Did the bishops repose more confidence in the effectiveness of treatment than do many people? Did we presume, perhaps too easily, that the Catholic people would appreciate the value of maintaining an ordained minister in the service of the church, if competent professionals said that he did not now pose a danger to anyone? Apparently we may have assumed too much, to judge by people's reaction to finding that same abusers were still in ministry even if they had been treated, their abuse now seemed firmly in the past, and they were offering effective service.

But the fact is, during the years when most national media found little interest in the issue of sexual abuse of minors by clergy, dioceses were continuing to confront this problem with programs such as background checks for all employees, even for volunteers, the introduction of safe environment programs, and making outreach to victims a part of their overall diocesan pastoral outreach. I mention these matters from the past, because they are the context in which the actions in Dallas need to be understood.

After several years of not being involved with the Ad Hoc Committee on Sexual Abuse, late last year I was asked by Bishop Wilton Gregory to be its chairman (U.S.C.C.B., "Restructured Committee on Sexual Abuse Announced"). It is a job I accepted because all of my experience as a bishop has demonstrated to me how important it is that the church deal with this issue and put this terrible problem behind us once and for all to the extent humanly possible.

I want to say emphatically that what the bishops did in Dallas was to build on an existing foundation of policies and pastoral outreach already in existence. However, the fact that there was so much ignorance of what bishops had already done, the fact the media could so misconstrue our past actions, and the fact that the Catholic people's confidence could be so shaken, all helped us to see the limitations of what we had been doing. Our actions in Dallas sought to offer improvements in our response deficiencies just as the Ad Hoc Committee in its very first action helped to strengthen diocesan policies by reviewing them all and suggesting improvements.

Among the improvements to our previous response made in Dallas has been to establish a set of national standards that makes it clear that the bishops are committed to a national solution to a national problem. Few among the general public seem to understand that the United States Conference of Catholic Bishops is not a governing body. It is an association of bishops intended to explore more unified pastoral responses to issues of common concern, but its deliberative power to make decisions binding on all bishops is very limited.

In the face of this dreadful crisis, there was a recognition of the need for a more proactive stance. The communiqué, issued last April at the end of the Interdicasterial meeting to which I referred above, says the United States participants "presented to the Prefects of the Roman Congregations" several proposals for action at our June general assembly ("Final Communiqué of Vatican-U.S. Church Leaders Summit," p. 771). The first one was, "We propose to send the respective Congregations of the Holy See a set of national standards which the Holy See will properly review (*recognitio*), in which essential elements for policies dealing with the sexual abuse of minors in Dioceses and Religious Institutes in the United States are set forth." (Ibid.)

We have done this; and, as we all know, the Holy See had asked for further reflection on and revision of some of our actions taken in Dallas.

This has been done. However, what the media took insufficient note of is that the Holy See is acting within the expectation set last April that the result of the process would be "a set of national standards." I think the latter concept is at the very core of what we did in Dallas to improve on the response we developed over the previous decade.

The purpose of these national standards is to assure a homogeneity of response to the problem. The standards provided in the Charter offer far more detail than the original five principles of what should comprise a diocesan response. Thus a clearer picture is provided of what a diocese that has made protection of children and young people a priority would do. We do not see this as an imposition on the dioceses, but as a way for each diocese to monitor its own response and to enable all dioceses to be accountable to one another. For many years now, the church's response overall to the sexual abuse problem has been judged not by the dioceses that have been handling these cases best but by those which have been deficient in handling them. A set of national standards is intended to maximize the response in every diocese.

The second improvement is the establishment of an Office for Child and Youth Protection (U.S.C.C.B., Statement of Monsignor William P. Fay, General Secretary, "On the Appointment of Ms. Kathleen McChesney as Executive Director of the Office for Child and Youth Protection"). The Ad Hoc Committee only temporarily had a full-time staff member to assist in its work. Its staff has primary obligations in other areas; and, of course, the bishop members have their own dioceses as their first obligation. By establishing this Office to help dioceses implement programs in this area and to do an annual assessment of how effectively they are dealing with the abuse issue in all its aspects, the bishops gave their commitment to the protection of children and young people a more solid organizational presence. I believe that if the Conference had been doing such assessments for the last several years, they would have provided the evidence of the many serious efforts to deal with this issue in our dioceses to rebut many of the distortions we read and heard during the past year.

The third and most controversial improvement has to do with the reassignment of priest abusers. Over the years, the discussion of reassignment has shown a variety of response among the bishops. Neither our theology nor Canon Law permits us to view priests as if they are mere employees. The charism of holy order, which no pope or bishop can take away nor any misconduct wipe out, has governed the bishop's hesitation to dismiss a priest abuser as he would a lay employee who commits sexual abuse. Bishops do view priests differently, but the reason for doing so is neither arbitrary nor sentimental. It is based on a firm foundation of faith and law.

In order to maintain ordained men in some relationship to the church, bishops have sent priest abusers to treatment centers which know the seriousness of their conditions and are not going to recommend that the priest be returned to priestly duties unless the indications are clear that he is not a danger to young people.

Genuine pedophiles–those attracted to prepubescent children–are not suitable for any ministry. Those attracted to older minors sometimes have less severe psychological problems which can be controlled with treatment, aftercare and monitoring. To be doubly sure, often this "ministry" has been a desk job that did not put the priest into contact with children.

These bishops also thought that maintaining these abusers in a setting where they could be monitored and were doing work for which they had been trained was a *safer* course for society than turning them out into the general population on their own. In this connection, I would like to clear up a misconception about reporting priests to authorities. With regard to law enforcement, there has been quite a change over the last several decades in the way child sexual abuse is handled by law enforcement. In the not so distant past, there was a sense that the matter should not be dealt with too publicly. It was ugly, and publicity was thought to have the potential of re-victimizing the child. As a result many cases went unprosecuted.

Thus there are many reasons for a priest or other perpetrators not to be prosecuted. Even if a priest is prosecuted and jailed, that is not the end of the story. Only laicization relieves a bishop of the obligation to a priest to provide suitably for him. If the priest does not voluntarily ask for it, a bishop still faces the question of how to deal with him. These complications are rarely known to the general public, much less understood by them.

However, re-assignment was not the only response. Some bishops, based on their experience, decided not to return any abuser to ministry and employed various canonical means to accomplish this.

What the bishops did in Dallas was to heed a clear message from a majority of our people that they were not secure with having in ministry even those priests who have received very effective treatment and who were being monitored.

During the last few months the bishops have now passed from being accused of protecting priest abusers to being accused of ignoring priests' rights. This is simplistic to the point of being false. To understand our actions in Dallas, one has to ask, "What is the pastoral experience of bishops?" It has been an experience of the pain of victims. My door has always been open to the victims. Their stories are horrendous and their suffering has been on-going. They are part of the Catholic family. I feel that to be true even if they have currently abandoned their faith because of what happened to them. No one can hear their stories without wanting to be able to assure them that everything is being done so that no other children will suffer such violation.

I have also spent much of my priesthood in priestly formation. The priesthood is very dear to me, and it has been extremely painful to see our good and faithful priests, who form the large majority, suffer on account of those who have done abominable things. As tragic as what has happened to victims, it is also tragic when priests who have served their people turn out to be men with a dark, compulsive, and predatory side. Parishioners have said, in great agony, that they will never believe that the man who visited their father faithfully in the hospital, brought Holy Communion to their grandmother on First Friday, and baptized their children could be the same man who committed the horrible violations they read about in the newspapers.

It is astonishing to me and a cause of great sadness that some of the men with whom we entrusted the most sacred mysteries used their unique vocation to satisfy their compulsions upon the most innocent among us. The church, which has never shirked from gathering the wounded stranger in her arms, cannot shirk from gathering the children wounded by her very own ministers.

This has been the bishops' pastoral experience–all these dimensions of pain with few if any false accusations occurring. The bishop cannot look at this situation only with the eyes of the priest. With psychological and spiritual empathy, he must look at the pain confronting him as much as he possibly can with the eyes of the victim and the eyes of the parent whose child has been molested.

The bishop cannot undo past harm, but he can work to make the environment of the church the safest of environments. We have been through a partial eclipse of the sun. What we know as so good, holy, and beautiful has had a shadow cast over it. We must allow the Sun of Justice, rising in our hearts with his healing rays, to inspire in us a commitment to relief for victims, protection for children, holiness and integrity in the life of priests, and courage and compassion in actions of bishops.

To change the metaphor, we called our document a charter because a charter is not a point of arrival but a map of how to get there. We have journeyed far since I began my own episcopal journey in Lafayette, but our old map was not as sure a guide as we thought. We have now drawn up another, and with God's help it will get us where we want to—where we must—be.

REFERENCES

"Final Communiqué of Vatican-U.S. Church Leaders Summit," *Origins*, Vol. 31, No. 46, May 2, 2002.

United States Conference of Catholic Bishops, "Charter for the Protection of Children and Young People Revised Edition, 2002." www. usccb.org/bishops/charter.htm.

United States Conference of Catholic Bishops, "Restructured Committee on Sexual Abuse Announced," (September 5, 2002). www.usccb.org/comm/archives /2002/ 02-170.htm.

United States Conference of Catholic Bishops, Statement of Monsignor William P. Fay, General Secretary, "On the Appointment of Ms. Kathleen McChesney as Executive Director of the Office for Child and Youth Protection." (June 3, 2003) www.usccb.org/comm/mcchespr.htm.

Trusting the Clergy:
A Response to Archbishop Harry J. Flynn

Michael J. Bland

SUMMARY. This essay is a direct response to Archbishop Harry J. Flynn's keynote at the Symposium "Trusting the Clergy: The churches and communities come to grips with sexual misconduct." It focuses on the context of the Catholic Church in the U.S., the experience of child victims of sexual abuse, and challenges the church to fulfill the "Charter for the protection of children and young people" presented by the U.S. Conference of Catholic Bishops. *[Article copies available for a fee from The Haworth Document Delivery Service: 1-800-HAWORTH. E-mail address: <docdelivery@haworthpress.com> Website: <http://www.HaworthPress.com> © 2003 by The Haworth Press, Inc. All rights reserved.]*

KEYWORDS. Archbishop Harry J. Flynn, clergy sexual abuse, Roman Catholic sex abuse crisis, US Conference of Catholic Bishops

I am grateful to have the opportunity to respond to Archbishop Flynn, who has been a leader, an implementer, an educator, and an author when it comes to addressing the sexual abuse crises in the church. At a recent meeting of the National Review Board, Monsignor Maniscalso, the Director of Communications for the United States Conference of

[Haworth co-indexing entry note]: "Trusting the Clergy: A Response to Archbishop Harry J. Flynn." Bland, Michael J. Co-published simultaneously in *Journal of Religion & Abuse* (The Haworth Pastoral Press, an imprint of The Haworth Press, Inc.) Vol. 5, No. 3, 2003, pp. 23-29; and: *Sexual Abuse in the Catholic Church: Trusting the Clergy?* (ed: Marie M. Fortune, and W. Merle Longwood) The Haworth Pastoral Press, an imprint of The Haworth Press, Inc., 2003, pp. 23-29. Single or multiple copies of this article are available for a fee from The Haworth Document Delivery Service [1-800-HAWORTH. 9:00 a.m. - 5:00 p.m. (EST). E-mail address: docdelivery@haworthpress.com].

http://www.haworthpress.com/web/JORA
© 2003 by The Haworth Press, Inc. All rights reserved.
Digital Object Identifier: 10.1300/J154v05n03_04

Catholic Bishops, lamented how awful 2002 had been for the church. He described the past year by referring to the lead character in the film *Groundhog Day*. "We've been through this already, read the stories, heard the names, and answered these questions." He went on to say that he expected that things could not get worse. At that point, board member Leon Panetta, former Chief of Staff for the Clinton White House, leaned forward, looked down the table and said, "With all due respect, Monsignor, my experience is that it can *always* get worse!"

The church has had a number of Groundhog Day experiences in the past twenty years as it has faced the issue of clerical sexual abuse of minors. This time it is different, however. The alarm is louder and the rebound is harder. Some people are struggling to view the newly promulgated "Charter for the Protection of Children and Young People" (USCCB, 2003) as a turning point in the history of the Church. Some have taken a "wait and see attitude." Others are publicly and privately calling the church to accountability and transparency. And still others, all be it sadly, have given up and walked away from the church. These varied responses help us appreciate the significance of the question posed in the title of this symposium: "Trusting The Clergy?" We can begin to respond to that question by asking a further question: What have we learned?

I shall first offer some context to help us understand the Catholic Church in the United States today. The Catholic Church is an enormous enterprise, not only internationally, but also here in the United States. According to the latest US census figures, more than 62 million Americans identify themselves as Catholic, nearly one in four of our national population. These Catholics are organized into 19,496 parishes in 195 dioceses across the country. According to the latest Catholic directory, the church maintains 238 colleges and universities, 1,343 high schools, 6,949 primary schools, 597 hospitals that served just over 82 million patients, 597 health care centers that treated nearly 6 million outpatients, and a total of 5,134 orphanages, day care facilities, and social service agencies that serve the poor and needy coast to coast (Kenedy, 2003). There are currently 45,713 priests in the United States within the 195 dioceses and approximately 355 male religious communities. Nearly 100,000 priests have served in the United States since 1960 (Kenedy, 2003).

I have cited these statistics to make a point about the nature and scope of the Catholic Church in the United States. The Catholic Church should not be identified simply by the actions of a few priests nor by the lack of action of a few bishops. It may be because of the behavior of a few priests or the lack of action by a few bishops that we have become all too familiar with headlines such as "The Church in Crisis" or "A Crisis without Precedent in Our Times," but the church is much more than what those headlines convey.

I find having a larger understanding of the church important, because it has been a meaningful part of my own healing. I was sexually abused by a priest and then hurt by a few religious leaders because they were unable to deal with this problem in an appropriate and responsible manner. But it was not "the church" that hurt me. Indeed for me, part of my healing has included availing myself of the rich and very diverse spiritual heritage and tradition of the Catholic Church offers. While some may say there are two sides to every story, I want to say when a minor is sexually abused by a priest there is only one reality that counts for that minor when he or she is sexually abused by a priest.

The problem of clerical sexual abuse of minors has been explained in a number of ways: inadequate psychosexual formation of priests, celibacy, homosexuality, priests not being allowed to marry, not allowing women priests, or priests not following church teachings. While these may be some of the background reasons that explain why a priest would abuse a minor, each of these explanations carries with it a different agenda. The main issue must remain clear: an adult, who happened to be a priest, sexually abused a minor. Therefore, the starting point must be removing that priest from ministry, and only then is it appropriate to begin looking at the possible causes that led him to engage in sexual abuse. Any other way of dealing with this begins to sound like rationalizations or excuses; even worse it runs the risk of re-victimizing the victim.

It is clear that for many years the problem of child sexual abuse in society was hidden from our view. However, in the past year, the problem of clergy sexual abuse of minors gained national and even international attention. We now know that child sexual abuse is not just a clergy issue and that it is not new. The phenomenon of child abuse has existed for centuries, but it was not until the 1970s that researchers began to focus their work specifically on understanding the extent of this phenomenon. As a result, in 1974, Congress passed the Child Abuse Prevention and Treatment Act, which mandated the reporting and investigation of abuse allegations, and similar measures were passed by all states with little opposition. In 1979, the United Nations gave additional visibility to the reality of child abuse when it sponsored the International Year of the Child.

Since the early 1980s the United States Conference of Catholic Bishops has had an Ad Hoc Committee to address the issue of clergy sex abuse. Over time, it made certain recommendations to the nation's bishops about what they could do in their own dioceses to make environments safer for children and youth. Many bishops followed these recommendations. Sadly, a number of bishops declined to implement these recommendations or improperly implemented these policies. The policies that the bishops' Ad Hoc Committee has recommended were never binding on any of the nation's bishops. By contrast, "The Charter for the Protection of Children and Young People" (USCCB, 2003) binds all the bishops of the United States to a uniform code of action and response in the event of accusations and instances of sexual abuse. I suggest that after being in existence for nearly 20 years, the Bishops Ad Hoc Committee on Sexual Abuses needs to be recognized as a permanent committee of the Unites States Conference of Catholic Bishops. There is nothing Ad Hoc about sexual abuse.

My knowledge of sexual abuse, aside from personal experience, comes from two major sources: popular recounting of incidents in the media and professional studies. In the past months, there has been a significant increase of coverage of sexual abuse in the popular media. Although such public exposure heightens our awareness of this problem, the facts are not easy to accept. To protect ourselves from this horror, we all too easily imagine that if sexual abuse does occur, it happens in another city, in a different social class, or to individuals who are, somehow, not like us. But we all know that none of this is true. Sexual abuse happens in all racial, ethnic, cultural, socioeconomic, and religious groups, and on all educational levels. The pervasiveness of the problem cannot be overstated.

Sexual abuse of minors refers to sexual acts occurring between a minor and an adult. Sexual abuse of a minor is the criminal, immoral, and sinful use of a minor as a sex object by an adult. The primary sexual activity of a child molester is usually exposing a minor to pornography, genital fondling, and masturbation. Intercourse is rare. Sexual contact tends to happen without overt force because the abuser/child molester has used grooming activities to desensitize the minor to wrongful sex. This grooming process involves the molester finding ways to "set up" the victim to make it easier for the abuser to offend. Grooming behaviors include gaining the victim's trust; luring the victim into seemingly innocent physical contact with the molester; making the victim feel indebted to the molester through gifts and/or special favors; making it emotionally difficult for the victim to resist; and confusing the victim about whether or not the sexual contact is acceptable. The behaviors often make the minor compliant and appear to be cooperative, giving the molester the illusion of the child's consent and justification for the crime. The molester's grooming of his victim is often a systematic seduction that wins the trust of a vulnerable and needy child.

It is very difficult for children to discuss the abuse that has happened to them. To discuss sexual issues is difficult for many people, but, to expect a child to discuss sexual issues, which he or she perceives as wrong, is even more difficult. This reality leaves the victim silent because of personal shame or guilt or because he or she was paralyzed by fears instigated by the child molester.

A few years ago, I conducted research involving five archdioceses and seven dioceses that identified seventy-three victim/survivors of sexual abuse. These victims/survivors each made a formal allegation of being sexually abused as a minor by a priest; the dioceses investigated their allegations and concluded that in each case there was reasonable cause to suspect that the allegation was credible. Of the seventy-three questionnaires that I sent out, forty-eight were returned, for a 65.7 percent return rate. The demographic results showed that the respondents ranged in age from 19 to 70. Fifty percent ($N = 24$) of the victims/survivors were female and fifty percent ($N = 24$) were male. Nearly 96 percent ($N = 46$) of the victims/survivors identified themselves as being raised Catholic; but when they were asked to identify their current religion, 73 percent ($N = 35$) identified themselves as Catholic, six percent ($N = 3$) identified themselves as Christian, two percent ($N = 1$) identified themselves as Non-Christian, and sadly 19 percent ($N = 9$) identified themselves as having no religion.

The victims of sexual abuse deserve our understanding and pledge that we as church will prevent what happened to them from happening to others. And the perpetrators, too, deserve our compassion and pledge to see to it that what they have done will neither be condoned nor permitted in any way to happen again. From my personal as well as my professional experience, I know healing of victims and perpetrators is possible.

Perhaps now in 2003 when sexual abuse has become a household term, it is a little easier for people to discuss sexual abuse issues, but it is still important for us to work to create an environment in which no one is paralyzed by fear. I hope it is a little easier for all sexual abuse victims to come forward now to "tell their story" as they search for psychological and spiritual healing. I hope also that it is a little easier for all sexual perpetrators to seek and find professional help.

All of this, I believe, destroys the hold that shame, hurt and deceit that sexual abuse can have on the victim, the perpetrator, and others. You know the old saying, "The cover-up is always worse than the crime." I suspect that generations of cover-ups generated a climate in which the evil and hurt of sexual abuse became closeted, and worse, not adequately understood. If there is anything that redeems this heartbreak and shame it is that the Catholic Church has had to face it, and it will end now.

In the Preamble to the "Charter" (USCCB, 2003), the bishops were blunt in acknowledging the sexual abuse of children by members of the clergy and the ways in which they had previously inadequately addressed these "crimes and sins" that brought such enormous "pain, anger, and confusion." In their apology, the bishops took full responsibility for failing victims in the past. They pledged to establish policies to prevent such failings in the future. These are enormous steps in the right direction, but there can be no wavering on the seriousness of this plan to safeguard children. Developing a healthy and safe church requires a firm commitment from all its members.

Admittedly, a bishop has a special canonical relationship with his priests. However, a bishop also has a special relationship with his flock, the faithful. And among his flock are those who have been sexually abused by a priest. For those who have been abused, the bishop must serve as their priest, pastor, shepherd, and healer. Such a relationship cannot be replaced by a legal process, attorneys or settlements. It is about being church to those who have been hurt by a priest, and being a representative of church and a reflection of that special canonical relationship lies with the bishop.

One of the most valuable things we, as church, can do help heal one another is to listen to each other's stories. From my personal and professional experience, I have come to understand that victims do not need or want anyone to feel sorry for them. They do not need to be patronized, pitied or told what to do. They need to feel that their pain, frustration, shame, anger, resentment, humiliation–their experience–is understood. They need empowerment to do what they need to do to find healing and wholeness for themselves. Survivors of abuse, like all of us, seek to have their feelings validated, acknowledged and perhaps, even for a moment, understood.

T. S. Eliot wrote: "We had the experience, but missed the meaning" (Eliot, 1939). Without stopping to reflect on an experience and seeking to understand it, the experience is merely an empty event. Things are different this time, I believe, as we, the church, better understand the experience and pain of the victims. It is not about finding the right words to move forward, nor is it about creating a strategy that will place us "out front" of an issue. It is about staying the course, it is about witnessing to the message of the Gospel, and it is about being church. It is about bringing about far-reaching structural changes that will create a safe environment for children and youth and that will create a system of transparency that will spare us from a return to this horrific nightmare. Words are good, but this time the words must be put into action in all dioceses and religious communities.

Like others, I am convinced that this is our last shot at getting this right. If we backslide, sidestep, or change the course, and settle for less than full accountability and complete transparency, we will fail because we will not get yet another chance. This time I hope we have finally learned that a person who has sexually abused a minor cannot be adequately supervised or monitored in the church. The church is a faith community not a therapeutic community. That is why today, if there is even one credible allegation of sexual abuse of a minor by a member of the clergy, he must be removed from ministry, and if the accusation is determined to be true, that priest should not be allowed to serve in public or internal ministry again.

As healing is possible for victims, so too is healing possible for secondary victims, including the church, the people of God. The church may need time for genuine lamentation, for the external expression of grief, brokenness and pain, for trembling and tears, for the very emotions and actions that often accompany mourning, repentance, forgiveness, and healing. Healing is not found in a deafening silence or empty words. There are no winners. And if, or when, a minor is sexually abused, we, the church, must respond immediately and deal with the sexual abuse in an appropriate and responsible manner.

REFERENCES

Bland, M.J. (2001). "The psychological and spiritual effects of child sexual abuse when the perpetrator is a catholic priest." *Dissertation Abstracts International*, 2002.

Eliot, T. S. (1939). *Old possum's book of practical cats*. London: Faber (1962).

Kenedy, P. J., & Sons. (2003). *The Official Catholic Directory*. New Providence, NJ: National Register Publishing.

United States Conference of Catholic Bishops. (2003). "Charter for the protection of children and young people." Washington, DC.

What Is the Agenda?
A Response to Archbishop Harry J. Flynn

Marie M. Fortune

SUMMARY. This essay is a direct response to Archbishop Harry J. Flynn's keynote at the Symposium "Trusting the Clergy: The churches and communities come to grips with sexual misconduct." It focuses on the contradiction between an institutional protection agenda and a justice-making agenda as seen in response to sexual abuse by Catholic priests. *[Article copies available for a fee from The Haworth Document Delivery Service: 1-800-HAWORTH. E-mail address: <docdelivery@haworthpress. com> Website: <http://www.HaworthPress.com> © 2003 by The Haworth Press, Inc. All rights reserved.]*

KEYWORDS. Clergy sexual abuse, Archbishop Harry J. Flynn, Roman Catholic sex abuse crisis

I appreciate the invitation to participate in this conversation. This opportunity for an open discussion of the particular crisis of sexual abuse in the Roman Catholic Church is long overdue and most welcome.

I come to this discussion as a Protestant pastor who has worked on the problem of sexual abuse by clergy for over twenty years. My early work was with the Archdiocese of Seattle developing training materials

[Haworth co-indexing entry note]: "What Is the Agenda? A Response to Archbishop Harry J. Flynn." Fortune, Marie M. Co-published simultaneously in *Journal of Religion & Abuse* (The Haworth Pastoral Press, an imprint of The Haworth Press, Inc.) Vol. 5, No. 3, 2003, pp. 31-34; and: *Sexual Abuse in the Catholic Church: Trusting the Clergy?* (ed: Marie M. Fortune, and W. Merle Longwood) The Haworth Pastoral Press, an imprint of The Haworth Press, Inc., 2003, pp. 31-34. Single or multiple copies of this article are available for a fee from The Haworth Document Delivery Service [1-800-HAWORTH, 9:00 a.m. - 5:00 p.m. (EST). E-mail address: docdelivery@haworthpress.com].

http://www.haworthpress.com/web/JORA
© 2003 by The Haworth Press, Inc. All rights reserved.
Digital Object Identifier: 10.1300/J154v05n03_05

on clergy abuse. Since January 2002, I have watched the unfolding disclosure of the situation in the Catholic Church with great sadness and despair. Let me assure you that no one in the non-Catholic community feels any joy whatever at this news. We stand in solidarity with those who suffer and with the wider church as it struggles to respond to this crisis. Let me also assure you that the problem of sexual abuse by clergy is one that we all share, and the media continue to report on cases among Protestants, Jews, Buddhists, and others. So be assured that my comments here are those of a loving critic, an outsider to the Catholic Church who believes in the church's capacity to do the right thing.

I appreciate Archbishop Flynn's comments and his efforts to provide leadership in the past ten years. The five principles he outlined are a solid foundation for an effective response to disclosure of sexual abuse. I know that there have been bishops all along who have tried to respond appropriately. And their efforts should not be overlooked. For example, this statement in 1995 from Bishop William G. Curlin of the Diocese of Charlotte, NC, exemplifies how a religious leader should respond to the abuse of children by priests. He went to the parish where Rev. William Kuder served in the 1950s and made this statement:

> Some may ask, 'Why bring this up now, after so many years following Father Kuder's death? What good can be accomplished by such a revelation?' Let me assure you that the victims of Father Kuder and their families have never ceased to feel the intense pain he brought them. Their Calvary has lasted a lifetime and continues to this day. . . . For those who were victims of Father Kuder, I assure you that you were innocent of all sin. You were a child who was abused and molested by a man who hid behind his priesthood and took advantage of it to use you for his personal pleasure. . . . We want to publicly apologize and declare our determination that this will never happen again. We as a Catholic community can allow no less than zero tolerance of this evil. (Reid, 1995)

Bishop Curlin emphasized the diocese's policy, which states that any allegation of sexual abuse against a priest will bring about his immediate removal from ministry pending an investigation and that any priest found guilty of sexual abuse will be expelled from the priesthood with no second chance (Reid, 1995).

I also agree with Archbishop Flynn that we need to acknowledge the places where there has been an informed, committed, and sensitive response. But at this point, the media have helped to expose a deep and abiding institutional crisis which cannot be minimized. I think what has been so difficult for so many is an overwhelming sense that the church hierarchy has not and does not understand what this is about. It is a question of agenda.

There are two agendas available in response to sexual abuse by clergy: an institutional protection agenda or a justice-making agenda. I think we can safely assume that the Gospel reflects a justice-making agenda.

An *institutional protection agenda* will use scripture to avoid action, e.g., "Do not judge so that you may not be judged," (Matthew 7:1 NRSV) It will use language to confuse and distort reality: "It was just an indiscretion and it only happened once." It will instruct its legal counsel to protect the church from victims and survivors. It will further develop policies whose sole purpose is to protect the institution from liability. It will urge liturgies in every diocese immediately focusing on forgiveness which will only serve to "heal the wound lightly . . . " (see Jeremiah 6:14). It will allocate its funds readily to defend the institution in civil litigation. It will look for a scapegoat and probably focus inappropriately on gay priests as the heart of the problem. It will shun victims and survivors and attempt to silence them. It will resist reform at all costs.

But the bishops have another choice of agendas, an agenda congruent with the teaching of the church. A *justice-making agenda* will use scripture to confront the sin and lift up victims, e.g., "It would be better for you if a millstone were hung around your neck and you were thrown into the sea than for you to cause one of these little ones to stumble." (Luke 17:2 NRSV). It will use language to clarify: "This is sexual abuse of the most vulnerable by the powerful. It is a sin and a crime." It will instruct its legal counsel to find ways to make justice for survivors and hold perpetrators accountable. It will develop and implement policies whose purpose is to protect the people from their institution and from those who would misuse their power. It will encourage liturgies, when the time is right, that name the sin, confess culpability, remember the victims, and celebrate justice really made–all of which makes for healing and restoration. It will allocate its funds for restitution for victims and survivors and for education and training for prevention. It will not look for a scapegoat but look inside itself with a critical eye focusing on power as the issue at stake here. It will seek out those who have been harmed, thank them for their courage in disclosing their abuse, and support them in their healing. It will have the courage to ask, what reforms do we need in order to be faithful to the Gospel?

Some bishops and cardinals have argued that their early management of the reports of priests' sexual abuse of children was sincerely motivated by their desire to protect the church from scandal. This translated as protecting priests from the consequences of their misconduct, keeping secrets, and limiting the financial liability of the institution. Ironically, their mismanagement now undermines the credibility of all priests, compromises the image and moral capital of the whole church, and will cost far more financially than it needed to. In other words, even the institutional protection agenda doesn't really protect the institution in the long run.

These longstanding cases of abuse by priests, silence, and cover up are all the evidence we need that the hierarchy of the church has been hijacked by those who chose the institutional protection agenda. Behind the façade of robes and incense, clerical privilege was allowed to trump the Gospel. And they have brought the church to the brink.

But the story is not over. The faithful few activists and survivors, bishops and bureaucrats, local priests and laity who are as appropriately outraged as Jesus was when he confronted the moneylenders in the temple, continue to stand witness and call upon the church to be the church. This is the leadership which actually believes that God calls us to stand with those who are most vulnerable, that making justice and healing are holy works, and that the church actually has the theological and spiritual resources to respond to this crisis.

With all due respect to Archbishop Flynn, I suggest that the institutional protection agenda is still holding sway in most dioceses. Hence we see church lawyers subpoenaing victims' psychotherapists and trying to use the First Amendment to have victims' suits dismissed in court.

The Gospel, not lawyers, should be guiding this process. The goal must be the protection of the vulnerable. The process must be fair and in concert with law enforcement when crimes have been committed. And the healing of survivors must take priority. Then the church can be the church.

REFERENCE

Reid, Tim, "Church Issues Apology," *The Asheville Citizen-Times*, March 6, 1995.

The Sexual Abuse Crisis:
What Have We Learned?
A Response to Archbishop Harry J. Flynn

Carolyn Moore Newberger

SUMMARY. This essay is a direct response to Archbishop Harry J. Flynn's keynote at the Symposium "Trusting the Clergy: The churches and communities come to grips with sexual misconduct." It focuses on what we know about abusers and their victims. *[Article copies available for a fee from The Haworth Document Delivery Service: 1-800-HAWORTH. E-mail address: <docdelivery@haworthpress.com> Website: <http://www. HaworthPress.com> © 2003 by The Haworth Press, Inc. All rights reserved.]*

KEYWORDS. Clergy sexual abuse, Roman Catholic sex abuse crisis

I come to this discussion as a psychologist and as a person raised in the Jewish tradition. I was first introduced to the reality of child sexual abuse in the church in a very unusual way. It was during the early 1970s when I was an intern in clinical child psychology in Boston. I had a close colleague who told me in the coffee room one day that he had been a priest, and had left the priesthood. I knew he was a devout Catholic, and asked, "Michael, why did you leave the priesthood?" He replied, "Well, I

[Haworth co-indexing entry note]: "The Sexual Abuse Crisis: What Have We Learned? A Response to Archbishop Harry J. Flynn." Newberger, Carolyn Moore. Co-published simultaneously in *Journal of Religion & Abuse* (The Haworth Pastoral Press, an imprint of The Haworth Press, Inc.) Vol. 5, No. 3, 2003, pp. 35-41; and: *Sexual Abuse in the Catholic Church: Trusting the Clergy?* (ed: Marie M. Fortune, and W. Merle Longwood) The Haworth Pastoral Press, an imprint of The Haworth Press, Inc., 2003, pp. 35-41. Single or multiple copies of this article are available for a fee from The Haworth Document Delivery Service [1-800-HAWORTH, 9:00 a.m. - 5:00 p.m. (EST). E-mail address: docdelivery@haworthpress.com].

http://www.haworthpress.com/web/JORA
© 2003 by The Haworth Press, Inc. All rights reserved.
Digital Object Identifier: 10.1300/J154v05n03_06

was assigned to a large city institution that took in boys from the streets, and I discovered that these boys were being taken in and were being molested by the members of the clergy and by the director of this institution. I couldn't reconcile that with my values and beliefs as a Catholic and as a priest. I had to go. I couldn't deal with it. I had to leave." And so, there's another fallout from these issues, which is the good men the churches have lost who otherwise would have been fine priests, as my friend Michael alternatively became a wonderful social worker in the lay world.

But why didn't I ask, "Michael, why didn't you tell someone?" I didn't ask Michael because in 1972 I didn't think to ask, and Michael, to my knowledge, didn't tell anyone in the church either.

This story can be seen as an indicator both of Michael's context and the culture in which he was embedded as a priest, where he couldn't or wouldn't tell, and also of the times. I was a young psychologist, just a few years from my degree. I was learning about children and adults, and mental illness and health, but I wasn't learning what I needed to ask, "Why didn't you tell?" But now I feel that there has been a process of growth, and development, of discovery and recognition.

In my comments I will try to give some sense of where I think the church and all of us need to go at this point. In his presentation, Archbishop Harry J. Flynn talked about looking through the eyes of the victims and the parents. I think he is right on target with that kind of expansion of the framework. As the Reverend Marie Fortune indicated, the church's institutional agenda is just not an adequate framework for understanding the problems you face or their solutions.

I would also argue that it is important to look through the eyes of abusers. Otherwise, you would have an imperfect sense of what you need to know to protect yourselves and the children that depend on you. Let us begin by looking at the world from the perspective of one who sexually abuses children. First, relinquish the idea that they look different from you or me. Anyone could molest children. They are often very nice people. "Niceness" is the best mask for an abuser to wear (De Becker, 1997, p. 56).

The majority of child sexual abusers are male. Most have fantasies about sex with children, and their inner lives are preoccupied with children. In fact, they become accomplished at living double lives. If they didn't, they couldn't trap children. If their motives were evident, they couldn't gain contact with children and acquire access to children, and enforce secrecy in their conduct of sex. These men are usually compulsively driven to have sex with children, and some, though not all, are sadistic and/or psychopathic. But they don't look it (Salter, 2003, p. 31)!

The church is an ideal setting for people who want access to children in order to prey on them. It is a community of trusting people, as are most communities of faith. These are communities in which our natural inclination is to trust in each other's goodness, good will, and shared values. For that reason, our guard is down and we don't recognize someone in our midst who might hurt our children.

The Catholic Church is also ideal because of the cover of celibacy. Does celibacy cause sexual abuse? I doubt it. But does an institution that is celibate provide a cover for someone who otherwise would not be interested in adult consensual sex? Absolutely.

The priesthood also provides authority and legitimacy. As a consequence, you have to assume that people who want access to children—people who seek opportunity, secrecy, and power and credibility with children in order to groom them for sexual relationships—will enter the priesthood.

In order to protect children, you have to assume that there will always be sexual abusers in the priesthood, despite your best efforts to screen them out. I will say more later about how you can better protect children from those who would prey on them, a problem not only in the church, but also in other high-risk institutions such as Big Brothers and Boy Scouts.

My husband, Dr. Eli Newberger, and I once consulted on a case of a pediatrician pedophile who offered his services to adolescents who had worries about their sexuality. Once he had them alone in his office, he masturbated the boys to ejaculation, and kept detailed records about each child. Does this mean that all pediatricians are pedophiles? Obviously not. It does mean that in order to protect children, a parent or a nurse should be in pediatricians' offices whenever they examine children (Newberger & Newberger, 1986).

We have to assume that pedophiles will be among us, and that we have to do what is necessary to make sure that they do not have opportunities to have access to children in order to exploit them.

Now let us think about what the world is like for children who have been abused by priests. In order to give you a sense of what the experience of victimization might be like for a child, I would like to tell you a hypothetical story. This story is about something I worry about every day, why I worry about it, and why it is important to worry about it. The story concerns Eli's and my grandson, Noah, who is five years old. Eli and I help take care of our two grandchildren, and often pick Noah up after his day in pre-kindergarten. I have recurring anxieties about being late. Noah knows when he comes out of his classroom that Baba and

Nana or Mommy or Daddy will be waiting for him. He lives in a world of safety, protection, and care, but he doesn't even think about being safe, protected, and cared for. It just happens. But what if, one day, Noah came out of the classroom and we were not there. What if he waited, and waited, and waited, and the teacher took him back into the classroom to wait some more after all the other children had been picked up, and still we didn't come. And what if we had had a flat tire and had been trying desperately to get there, but couldn't in time. And finally, one-half hour later, we rushed into the classroom and picked up Noah. This has never happened to Noah, but it is my recurrent worry.

If this were to happen, in that one-half hour Noah's whole worldview would have changed. It would have fundamentally, seismically shifted. Noah would no longer be innocently operating in a world in which he is safe, in which adults are predictably there, in which he is reliably picked up, nourished and protected. He would now be in a world where he cannot trust that when he gets out of that classroom, someone will be there. Such a seismic shift is what occurs when someone has been in a world in which he or she has been cared for, and all of a sudden discovers that bad things can happen in that good world. We are not referring to bad things like being punished for stealing cookies out of the cookie jar, but bad things in the very fabric of a child's sense of safety, the very fabric of the meaning of people and places in the child's life.

Such a seismic shift happens when children are sexually abused–by anyone. Their worldview changes, and it makes them untrusting, fearful, and anxious. It can take a long time to win back a child's trust, and trust never returns entirely. The child has learned something fundamental, which is that trustworthiness cannot be taken for granted. This represents a level of cognitive awareness that did not exist before the abuse. Now the child realizes, "Things can go wrong and I have to watch out" (Dodge, Bates, & Pettit, 1990). Now these are lessons that everyone learns sooner or later, but you don't want children to learn them through trauma; you want them to learn them through appropriate, educative means.

Unlike the normal lessons children learn, and the lessons children learn from the trauma of natural disasters, sexual abuse comes wrapped in other layers of trauma. One is the layer of betrayal. Child sexual abuse is usually defined as sexual contact with someone five years or more older than the child, someone that a child would naturally assume would protect rather than harm (Finkelhor, 1979). Child abuse that takes place within the family is a particularly harmful betrayal, because it shatters the assumption that people who take care of them, who purport to love them won't hurt them. Not only do sexually abused children learn that they can no longer trust that they will be predictably safe and protected, they also learn that people they rely on may actually intend to harm them (Freyd, 1998).

That childhood abuse can cause grave psychological harm is no longer doubted by professionals in the field (e.g., Ackerman, Newton, McPherson, Jones, & Dykman, 1998; Boney-McCoy & Finkelhor, 1996; Collings, 1995; Jumper, 1995; Neumann, Houskamp, Pollock, & Briere, 1996; Newberger, & De Vos, 1988; Newberger & Gremy, in press; Newberger, Gtemy, Waternaux, & Newberger, 1993; Polusny & Follette, 1995). Recent research also reveals that childhood abuse changes the brain in ways that enduringly compromise emotional stability (Cromdie, 2003).

The church is also a place that takes care of people, where children experience and believe in the love of that church and its members for them, and by extension, the love of God for them. What is different about clergy abuse is that it shatters not only trust in the behavior and intentions of those who give care to children, but also trust in the systems of beliefs that give children a sense of meaning and community in their lives.

What are the effects of abuse by a priest? Levels of betrayals of that magnitude can make its victims feel and be pretty irrational. It can create in different people confusion, guilt, fear, intrusive dreams or recollections, jumpiness and irritability, difficulties concentrating, suspicions of the intentions of others, physical symptoms, feelings of worthlessness, and depression. If a person is vulnerable to unwanted and intrusive re-experiencing of the abuse, and his or her functioning is threatened by the disruptive symptoms that so frequently accompany trauma, that person is simultaneously going to try to avoid people, objects, and settings that will trigger those symptoms (Kendall-Tackett, Williams, & Finkelhor, 1993; March & Anaya-Jackson, 1993).

Many of you may have been puzzled by some victims' responses to being interviewed, for example, in church chanceries. Given what we have just discussed, if you put yourself in their shoes, you cannot assume that a setting in which you derive comfort and meaning is also going to be a setting in which they can feel comfortable, or even emotionally safe. And so, let us return to Archbishop Flynn's focus on putting yourself in the eyes of victims and the eyes of parents, who have experienced betrayal, too, through the church's abuse of their children. Those who would reach out to victims need continually to be monitoring and asking, "What would be best for you? We would like to reach out to you. Would you welcome that, or is that something you don't feel ready for right now? Will you let me know if and when you feel ready? Would you like to speak with me? On what terms would that be most comfortable for you?"

Not just the church, but anyone who deals with victims that come from an environment in which people have been betrayed, needs always to be respectful of where they are coming from, and to understand that the loss of trust that is inherent in being victimized means that there may also be a loss of trust in what you hold most fundamental. That loss of trust must be respected, and perhaps at some future point that trust may be restored. But it will not re-emerge if you tell them what they should believe, how they should feel, or how they should behave. Trust can only re-emerge if you can show them that you can hear how trust for them has been breached.

I would like to end with a comment that I heard this morning from Father Dennis Tamburello. When Father Tamburello picked us up this morning, he told us that he has a prison ministry. Unbeknownst to him when he began this ministry, his predecessor was one of the priests accused of molesting children. As a consequence, the inmates did not trust Father Tamburello. They had not been abused themselves by the priest that he replaced, but their trust in Father Tamburello was shaken by the fact that they had trusted someone who was untrustworthy. Father Tamburello's response to the inmates was, "Well, I'll have to earn your trust."

REFERENCES

Ackerman, P.T., Newton, J.E.O., McPherson, W.B., Jones, J.G., & Dykman, R. "Prevalence of post traumatic stress disorder and other psychiatric diagnoses in three groups of abused children (sexual, physical, and both)". *Child Abuse & Neglect*, 1998. 22: 759-774.

Boney-McCoy, S., & Finkelhor, D. "Is youth victimization related to trauma symptoms and depression after controlling for prior symptoms and family relationships? A longitudinal, prospective study." *Journal of Consulting and Clinical Psychology*, 1996. 64: 1406-1416.

Collings, S.J. "The long-term effects of contact and noncontact forms of child sexual abuse in a sample of university men." *Child Abuse and Neglect*, 1995. 19: 1-6.

Cromdie, W.J. "Childhood abuse hurts the brain." *Harvard University Gazette*, May 22, 2003, page 1.

De Becker, G. *The Gift of Fear*, Boston: Little-Brown, 1997.

Dodge, K.A., Bates, J.E., & Pettit, G.S. "Mechanisms in the cycle of violence." *Science*, 1990, 250: 1678-1683.

Finkelhor, D. *Sexually Victimized Children*. New York, Free Press, 1979.

Freyd, J. *Betrayal Trauma*, Cambridge, MA, Harvard University Press, 1998.

Jumper, S. "A meta-analysis of the relationship of child sexual abuse to adult psychological adjustment." *Child Abuse and Neglect*, 1995, 19: 715-728.

Kendall-Tackett, K.A., Williams, L.M., & Finkelhor, D. "Impact of sexual abuse on children: A review and synthesis of recent empirical studies," *Psychological Bulletin*, 1993, 113, 164-180.

March, J.S., & Amaya-Jackson, L. "Post-traumatic stress disorder in children and adolescents." *PTSD Research Quarterly*, 1993, 4: 1-7.

Neumann, D.A., Houskamp, B.M., Pollock, V.E., & Briere, J. The long-term sequelae of childhood sexual abuse in women: A meta-analytic review. *Child Maltreatment*, 1996, 1: 6-16.

Newberger, C.M., & De Vos, E. Abuse and victimization: A life-span developmental perspective. *Am J Orthopsychiat*, 1988: 58: 505-511.

Newberger, C.M., & Gremy, I. The role of clinical and institutional interventions in children's resilience and recovery from sexual abuse, In Clauss-Ehlers, *Child Resilience and Cultural Competence*, Temple University Press, in press.

Newberger, C.M., Gremy, I.M., Waternaux, C.M., & Newberger, E.H. Mothers of sexually abused children: Trauma and repair in longitudinal perspective, *American Journal of Orthopsychiatry,* 1993, 63: 92-102.

Newberger C.M., & Newberger E.H. When the pedophile is a pediatrician. In: Burgess, N.W., ed. *Sexual exploitation by health professionals.* New York, NY: Praeger, 1986, 99-106; reprinted in: Maney, A., ed. Professionals and the sexual abuse of children: Public health approaches. New York, NY: Praeger, 1988, 65-72.

Polusny, M.A., & Follette, V.M., Long-term correlates of child sexual abuse: Theory and review of the empirical literature. *Applied and Preventive Psychology,* 1995, 4:143-166.

Salter, A.C., *Predators, Pedophiles, Rapists, and Other Sex Offenders.* New York, NY: Basic Books, 2003.

Keynote:
The Sexual Abuse Crisis:
What Issues Do We Still Have to Face?

Donald B. Cozzens

SUMMARY. Fr. Cozzen's keynote at the "Trusting the Clergy?" Symposium takes a critical and constructive view of the Catholic sexual abuse crisis. He examines "What have we learned?" and "What do we still have to face?" by looking at issues of accountability, transparency, and the role of laity. *[Article copies available for a fee from The Haworth Document Delivery Service: 1-800-HAWORTH. E-mail address: <docdelivery@haworthpress.com> Website: <http://www.Haworth Press.com> © 2003 by The Haworth Press, Inc. All rights reserved.]*

KEYWORDS. Donald B. Cozzens, clergy sexual abuse, Roman Catholic sex abuse crisis

It is a privilege to participate in this important and timely symposium. In spite of strong voices to the contrary, I'm convinced that we need to face the tragic subject of today's conference with candor and courage. Yet, in spite of the expansive media coverage generated by clergy sexual abuse, relatively few conferences addressing the issue

[Haworth co-indexing entry note]: "Keynote: The Sexual Abuse Crisis: What Issues Do We Still Have to Face?" Cozzens, Donald B. Co-published simultaneously in *Journal of Religion & Abuse* (The Haworth Pastoral Press, an imprint of The Haworth Press, Inc.) Vol. 5, No. 3, 2003, pp. 43-52; and: *Sexual Abuse in the Catholic Church: Trusting the Clergy?* (ed: Marie M. Fortune, and W. Merle Longwood) The Haworth Pastoral Press, an imprint of The Haworth Press, Inc., 2003, pp. 43-52. Single or multiple copies of this article are available for a fee from The Haworth Document Delivery Service [1-800-HAWORTH, 9:00 a.m. - 5:00 p.m. (EST). E-mail address: docdelivery@haworthpress.com].

http://www.haworthpress.com/web/JORA
© 2003 by The Haworth Press, Inc. All rights reserved.
Digital Object Identifier: 10.1300/J154v05n03_07

have been held. The conveners of our symposium are to be congratulated. I hope more conferences like this one are being planned.

The faith community has suffered a serious, scandalous wound. If we are to set upon healing this wound, we have to know its true nature, its depth, and its scope. As we will see, there is significant resistance to such a probing examination–especially on the part of some "doctors of the soul," on the part of some church leaders.

THE SEXUAL ABUSE CRISIS: WHAT HAVE WE LEARNED?

At the start, let me say that we have indeed learned a number of painful lessons since the clergy sexual abuse scandal broke wide open–again and again and again.

- We have learned, perhaps imperfectly, that we must put the spiritual and personal welfare of those wounded ahead of everything else, including the welfare of our respective institutions.
- We have learned to respond in a more pastoral fashion in the past months and years. It is sad and telling reality that we church people had to learn this lesson.
- We have tried to reach fair settlements with those our clergy–and other church personnel–have wounded.
- We have worked hard to put in place administrative policies to ensure proper and prompt responses to allegations of sexual misconduct.

These are significant lessons learned. Significant strides have been made. We have indeed learned much that is important–and humbling. While our credibility has been greatly diminished and our trustworthiness has been severely weakened, we church leaders and administrators have, I believe, grown spiritually in the process of responding to so many cries of pain and betrayal.

THE SEXUAL ABUSE CRISIS: WHAT ISSUES STILL NEED TO BE FACED?

Concern for the Victims

Have we given sufficient thought to the on-going pastoral care of victims and their families? Some dioceses believe that a year or so of counseling for victims of clergy abuse should be sufficient. Determining what is appropriate therapeutic support for the abused remains a thorny issue for church authorities. Pastoral visits from bishops and other church leaders are critically important. Yet, early on many Catholic bishops were advised by their legal counsel not to meet with victims. Financial settlements, of course, will continue to be of critical importance. So the question looms: How will we minister to and support abuse victims in the months and years ahead? Do we have the resources and the will to provide on-going pastoral care and support that is likely to be needed at least in a number of cases?

Who will carry the day when future allegations of abuse come to our chanceries and church offices? Who will set the tone, and shape the administrative decisions that are proving so vitally important for all involved? Will it be the attorneys? Or will it be the shepherds? In too many cases from my own tradition, the attorneys have had the last word. In our efforts to protect our resources and to avoid scandal, we Catholics have often caused a greater scandal by putting the reputation of the church and the priesthood ahead of the welfare of those who have been so terribly wounded. What meaningful role will non-ordained men and women, especially parents, have in setting this tone and shaping administrative policies?

Concern for the Churches' Mission

Most, if not all, of the churches represented here today are churches of the Word. Our mission is to bring the saving, healing, liberating Word of God to a society and culture that appears profoundly confused about what really matters. We believe we have a Word from the Lord, a word that is desperately needed in the first years of this new millennium.

With our credibility diminished and our trustworthiness compromised, can we find ways to regain the trust and confidence we enjoyed in previous times? If we cannot, our preaching of the Word of God is likely to fall on distracted, if not deaf ears. Not only our own congregations, but society at large, are saying to us: "Physician, heal thyself before you speak of healing and salvation."

In my own tradition, it is not enough, nor is it prudent, to remind people that only a small percentage of clergy and church personnel have sexually abused. For the wound of sexual abuse has been further deepened by the administrative bungling—and that is putting it kindly—that has been the hallmark of many Catholic dioceses. One of the major issues still to be faced, then, is the critical issue of integrity. Unless church leaders and preachers of the Word are men and women of integrity–and perceived as people of integrity–the mission of the church is compromised.

Transparency and Accountability

We hear a good deal these days about transparency and accountability. If the integrity of church leaders is to be regained, we might begin by calling for greater transparency and real accountability. Let me mention some concrete examples from my own tradition.

Transparency

We Catholics still do not know the scope of the clergy abuse of minors and children because we do not know the number of credible allegations brought against deacons, priests, and bishops. I am not talking about names, I'm talking about numbers. We still don't know what percentage of clergy are abusers. In the majority of U.S. Catholic dioceses, we don't know the number of abusers in relation to the number of active clergy. How does the percentage of clergy abusers compare to percentage of abusers in the population at large? We don't know if there is a difference in the percentage of abusers between married and celibate clergy, between so-called high church clergy and evangelical clergy? Until we understand the scope–and nature–of the scandal, our efforts to address it will be misguided and ineffective.

Why are we so reluctant to reveal the actual scope of the problem? Are we afraid of further scandal? Are we afraid that an already wounded church will be further wounded? Are we afraid that the discipline of mandatory celibacy for diocesan priests of the Latin rite will be challenged even more than it is presently? We seem to have failed to learn, with notable exceptions, that the scope of the scandal will eventually come out. The sooner the true extent of the abuse becomes generally known, the better off all parties will be.

No one, of course, wants to exaggerate the problem. Yet church officials would be naïve to think that there are not numerous incidents of clergy misconduct with minors and children that have not come to their attention. Most victims of clergy abuse never come forward. William Reid, writing in a 1988 essay in *The Psychiatric Times,* claims that "careful studies have indicated . . . that child molesters commit an average of sixty offenses for every incident that comes to public attention" (Reid, 1988).

No doubt a certain institutional denial is understandable. It is the common temptation of leaders of government, business, and education. Succumbing to the temptation, church leaders, instead of wrestling with admittedly difficult questions that often escape even partial, tentative answers, emphasized that the problem of clergy abuse with minors and children was simply a slice of a broader social problem; they pointed out that most pedophiles were married men; and predictably, that there is a higher incident rate for this kind of abuse among teachers, coaches, scout leaders, and other professionals who work with youngsters. We are given the impression that clergy abuse is the result of a few bad apples in an otherwise healthy barrel. Until we know the facts of the matter, such claims and disclaimers are subject to considerable skepticism.

Many Catholics today are asking church authorities for the actual financial cost of the scandal. They are coming to see that the resources of the diocese are *their* resources. Since it is their money, they want to know where it goes and how decisions are made to allocate it. These Catholic men and women believe they have a right to such information. They are not satisfied with media reports of settlements and awards to victims. They expect a full financial report from their dioceses relating to the costs of the scandal. Court ordered awards and private settlements receive the most attention. But other costs are often overlooked: the cost of assessment and treatment of the clergy offender; the cost of counseling for the victim and his or her family; the cost of legal counsel; the cost of public relations firms. Many are conservatively estimating the scandal's cost to the Catholic Church as now over a billion dollars. And there are mountains of civil suits waiting to be processed.

Accountability

Adult believers are coming of age. They understand now that for some time in some of our churches they have not been treated as adults. Members of our congregations are well educated and quite articulate. They look for compelling biblical and theological rationales behind the doctrines and practices put forward by their bishops and pastors. And they are expecting appropriate accountability from their church leaders. It is a common understanding that accountability in the Catholic Church has traditionally been upward–priests are accountable to their bishops and bishops are accountable to the pope. Seldom does one hear of a priest apologizing to his people for a mistake in judgment or behavior. Almost never do we hear of a bishop apologizing to his priests. This hierarchical order, it was thought, was divinely constituted.

Since the Vatican Council, however, Catholics understand that through the Sacrament of Baptism they are full and equal members of the church even though their function and role as church members are quite different from that of priest or bishop. Such an understanding of their role has led them to see that, at least in the past and in many cases even now, they have been and are treated as less than adults when accountability issues are raised. The anger, even rage, expressed by Catholics of many different ideological stripes over the bishops mishandling of priest abusers of children and minors has signaled a most significant change in the attitude of Catholics vis-a-vis church authority. The day has passed when it was assumed that "Father knows best."

In my own tradition, some bishops are asked, "Why did you reassign a priest abuser to another parish without at least informing the new parish of his baggage? Why did you write testimonial letters for a priest abuser to allow him to be accepted by another diocese?" "What were you thinking," the laity ask, "especially in the middle and last years of the 1990s when you understood the compulsive nature of sexual abuse?"

Catholics are watching to see if the United States Conference of Bishops will give the Keating Commission the on-going financial support and cooperation it needs to fulfill its mandate of insuring the norms of the Dallas meeting are followed. This kind of accountability to the faithful is good and appropriate. And it is likely to be demanded if it is not forthcoming.

The Issue of Meaning

The members of the therapeutic, healing professions contributing to this discussion know the importance of seeking to understand the meaning behind violent and destructive behaviors. Many church denominations seem content to use crisis management when an allegation erupts in the media. They work hard: to respond pastorally to the alleged victims; to issue press statements summarizing the known facts of the allegation; to meet with church members distraught by the charges brought against their pastor; to consult with attorneys; to arrange for the necessary assessment of the accused pastor; to make appropriate reports to the civil authorities; and to conduct their own internal investigation of the allegation. In the heat of the moment, most church leaders try their hardest to respond to the crisis reasonably and responsibly.

But we need to go beyond sound pastoral responses to clergy abuse. We need to probe what's going on at deeper levels–we need to wrestle with the meaning of the behavior. Here again, I need to speak from my own Catholic tradition.

A number of commentators believe that the debacle of clergy sexual misconduct with minors and children is revealing more than the human frailty and pathology of a relatively small number of priests, pastors, and bishops. They propose that the crisis is pointing to a cancer in the very systemic structure of the ministry and hierarchy. By *systemic structure* they mean those ecclesial patterns of communication, operation, and discipline that both define the lives of the minister and facilitate their exercise of authority and power. It includes an almost infinite number of cues, signs, and symbols of identity and power that constitute the present clerical and hierarchical culture of the Catholic world.

Is it not possible, they reason, that the problem of priests' sexual contact with minors, while tragic in its own right, is more than an overflow of a societal problem into the ranks of priests and bishops? Priests are human, the defense goes, some will have a problem with alcohol, others with money and possessions, and some will be sexually attracted to children and teenagers. According to this line of thinking, it's a human, moral problem, not a systemic problem. This kind of analysis offers consolation and a useful rationalization for those who find the present clerical system compatible with their personal needs, with those who feel the rightness of the system as the clear gift of the Spirit, and with those who feel compelled, out of a sense of ecclesial loyalty, to uphold the current system without critical reflection.

Defenders of the present Catholic, ecclesial structure see probes such as the kind I am proposing here as subversive of the priesthood itself and as thinly disguised attempts to change the present practice and discipline of the church, especially the discipline of mandated celibacy for Latin rite diocesan priests. An open, mature church, one would think, would welcome reflection and discussion on its policies, practices, and disciplines, especially when these structures may shed light on the causes and meaning of the present scandal. These are not matters of revelation or doctrine. Furthermore, to insist as some are doing that there is simply no correlation between mandated celibacy and the present scandal in the Catholic Church–without full knowledge about the scope of the crisis–seems disingenuous. For some time now, Catholics have been directed by the highest Vatican sources to refrain from publicly discussing the issue of mandated celibacy. Clearly, this Vatican directive is not being followed.

Still, we need to ask if there is something at work in the ministerial calling and its culture–and in the case of the Catholic Church, mandated celibacy–that contributes to the kind of psycho-sexual immaturity that has been linked to the abuse of teens and children. We need to examine how ministers of the Word of God can rationalize, often without seeming remorse, their sexually abusive behavior with our young. Consider the incident reported by the English writer John Cornwell in his book, *Breaking Faith*. Cornwell writes,

> Not long before he died, one of my close priest friends who had a position of responsibility as chaplain in a Catholic residential college told me on his sixty-ninth birthday that he was currently attempting to seduce an eighteen-year-old male student into a sexual liaison. Wise and evidently good in countless ways, he was a stirring preacher and a man who loved his priesthood, but I came to see that his life was profoundly dislocated. I realized that although I had been acquainted with him for twenty-five years, I hardly knew him at all. He said, "I'm convinced that I cannot become fully human until I've had sexual relations with this young man." At one point he said, "Oh, the body is just a playground; it's the soul that matters." (Cornwell, 2001, pp. 146-47)

Church authorities have yet to study carefully the rationalizations of abusers and their understanding of chastity and celibacy. The results of such studies, I'm convinced, would be disturbing, perhaps profoundly disturbing, yet essential to any long-term resolution to the present scandals.

Still other questions come to mind. Would our denial have gone unchecked if victims had not organized and news reporters had not persisted in their investigations and judges had not ordered the unsealing of church documents and records relating to sexual abuse? How is it that church officials regularly denied or minimized the harm done to our children? How is it that we put the welfare of the institutional church ahead of the welfare of our young? These are some of the most urgent questions and issues that still need to be faced.

Why the Resistance?

Earlier I mentioned that denial, minimization, and resistance are part and parcel of the human condition. It is not strictly speaking an ecclesial problem. It is a human problem. I believe, nonetheless, that these forms of denial are more egregious in church polities because our churches claim to be speaking for the revealed Word of God. As custodians of the tradition and preachers of revealed Truth, we have every right to expect our pastors and ministers, our diocesan and jurisdictional leaders, to be truthful and candid. When they are less than truthful and candid, church leaders weaken the very fabric of the church, compromise its mission, and heap scandal upon scandal.

Perhaps it is felt in some quarters that if the churches are candid and forthcoming about the various issues I have raised here the churches would be giving ammunition to their enemies. My point is that we are giving ammunition to our enemies when we are not candid and forthcoming about the present scandal. The church's critics have been feasting on the abundant follies of church leaders for more than a year now. Moreover, we offend again the victims of abuse and their families by trying to put the best possible face on our present situation.

CONCLUSION

Most of the issues I've addressed here are related directly or indirectly to the role of church leaders and church authorities. I have addressed these issues, with your understanding, I trust, from my perspective as a Catholic priest. Time has not permitted the treatment of a number of important issues such as the role of power in sexual misconduct, the screening process for ministry candidates, and the on-going education and formation of our ordained leaders. It seems, nonetheless, that one last issue needs to be raised if ever so briefly: the role of lay women and men in coming to grips with sexual misconduct.

The laity may well step up and assume their birthright as full, adult members of their respective churches. Here, I believe, under the abiding presence of God's Spirit, lies the hope of the future. No doubt their emerging voice and influence will threaten a good number of church leaders and be perceived by some as a major threat to the hegemony of the institutional church.

Lay women and men, of course, like their ordained conferees, are both saints and sinners, subject to the same human weaknesses we now see so clearly in clergy and other church leaders. They seem, nonetheless, to be anointed at this precarious juncture in the church's history to offer the leadership and vision so wanting in many of our ecclesial assemblies. They deserve to be heard, respected, and encouraged. I believe they are God's gift to our troubled churches.

An unholy silence is being broken by conferences like this one. We are moving, if ever so slowly, from a culture of silence and secrecy to a culture of conversation, consultation, and collaboration. Let me conclude with the final sentences from *Sacred Silence: Denial and the Crisis in the Church.*

> Without healthy dialogue, the denial and "church spins" marking the first years of the present century will continue to threaten the integrity and credibility of our bishops and the very mission of the church. It is time to replace fear with confidence and control with trust. It is time for a holy silence and a sacred listening. Above all, it is time for courageous, honest speech–a time to tell the truth in love. (Cozzens, 2003, p. 172)

REFERENCES

Cornwell, John. (2001) *Breaking Faith: The Pope, the People, and the Fate* (New York: Viking Compass).

Cozzens, Donald (2003) *Sacred Silence: Denial and The Crisis in the Church* (Collegeville, MN: Liturgical Press).

Reid, William H., "The Psychiatric Times," April 24, 1988, quoted in A. W. Richard Sipe, *Sex, Priests, and Power: Anatomy of a Crisis* (New York: Brunner/Mazel, 1995), 25.

Ethics and Legalities:
A Response to Fr. Donald B. Cozzens

Marie M. Fortune

SUMMARY. This essay is a direct response to the keynote by Fr. Cozzens at the Symposium "Trusting the Clergy: The churches and communities come to grips with sexual misconduct," discussing the emphasis in recent responses by dioceses which seems to focus on avoiding legal liability and offering an ethical analysis of sexual abuse by clergy. *[Article copies available for a fee from The Haworth Document Delivery Service: 1-800-HAWORTH. E-mail address: <docdelivery@haworthpress.com> Website: <http://www.HaworthPress.com> © 2003 by The Haworth Press, Inc. All rights reserved.]*

KEYWORDS. Donald B. Cozzens, clergy sexual abuse, Roman Catholic sex abuse crisis, sexual abuse and ethics, sexual abuse and legal liability

Every morning I begin my day by checking the current compilation of news articles on clergy abuse which appear on my email. Usually there are 10-12 new articles, mostly describing new cases being prosecuted or civil actions initiated or the latest diocesan attempt to maneuver its way out of liability. Every day.

[Haworth co-indexing entry note]: "Ethics and Legalities: A Response to Fr. Donald B. Cozzens." Fortune, Marie M. Co-published simultaneously in *Journal of Religion & Abuse* (The Haworth Pastoral Press, an imprint of The Haworth Press, Inc.) Vol. 5, No. 3, 2003, pp. 53-58; and: *Sexual Abuse in the Catholic Church: Trusting the Clergy?* (ed: Marie M. Fortune, and W. Merle Longwood) The Haworth Pastoral Press, an imprint of The Haworth Press, Inc., 2003, pp. 53-58. Single or multiple copies of this article are available for a fee from The Haworth Document Delivery Service [1-800-HAWORTH, 9:00 a.m. - 5:00 p.m. (EST). E-mail address: docdelivery@haworthpress.com].

http://www.haworthpress.com/web/JORA
© 2003 by The Haworth Press, Inc. All rights reserved.
Digital Object Identifier: 10.1300/J154v05n03_08

THE CHURCH'S MISSION: AVOID LIABILITY

One of the most disturbing pieces of news in the recent fallout from the sex abuse scandals in the Roman Catholic Church is the revelation of a change in legal strategy on the part of the Church. The Washington Post reported (5/13/02):

> Where once the church tried to quietly settle cases, according to church and plaintiff lawyers, it is now pursuing an aggressive litigation strategy, hiring high-powered law firms and private detectives to examine the personal lives of the church's accusers, fighting to keep documents secret and engaging in new tactics to minimize settlements.

The "church's accusers" are adult survivors of sexual abuse at the hands of pedophile priests–priests whom it appears were protected from legal consequences, retained in ministry with the knowledge of their superiors, and moved from parish to parish. The result is a list of hundreds of children abused by someone they were taught to trust.

If this were any other institution, the contradiction would not be so profound. But this is the church–supposedly the faithful followers of Jesus who said, "Let the little children come to me, and do not stop them; for it is to such as these that the kingdom of heaven belongs" (Matthew 19:14 NRSV). Thus one has to wonder, who is running these dioceses? It sounds like the lawyers are in charge and scripture and theology be damned.

It has been a longstanding problem in every denomination and movement: the religious leadership whose responsibility it is to oversee the institution handing the problem of sexual abuse by clergy over to lawyers. Many lawyers for judicatories have seen their job as "protecting their clients," e.g., the diocese, from legitimate complaints by congregants. Sadly this approach has been short sighted at best and immoral at worst.

Not reporting allegations of child abuse to authorities, secret settlements which place gag orders on survivors, harassment of complainants, retention of pedophile priests and no notification of the parishes in which they serve–these are the outcomes for which dioceses have paid a high price to lawyers. None of this serves the interests of the church or its members.

Bishops need the skills of lawyers to help judicatories respond to complaints of sexual abuse by clergy. Bishops can direct their lawyers to develop and implement policies and procedures whose purpose is to stop abusers, identify victims, and bring healing to them and their families. Lawyers can help a diocese respond carefully in investigating and adjudicating complaints and in responding compassionately to victims and survivors. They can help make justice for those who have been harmed and justice leads to healing. Lawyers can help the church be the church. Instead all too often lawyers have helped the church forget it is the church.

A justice-making response is actually in the best interest of their client, the diocese. It is consistent with the stated values of the institution. It addresses a very real internal problem of misconduct and seeks to limit its impact. It ultimately saves money and protects the financial and moral assets of the institution. This is why the current news of an even more aggressive legal strategy designed to keep secrets and avoid the financial consequences of misconduct and mismanagement is so disturbing. Have they not learned anything from this tragic history?

If the Roman Catholic Church persists in this aggressive legal strategy, it will continue to reap what it sows. Perhaps at least it could post a sign in every parish entrance: "WARNING: We are not responsible for any harm that your priest may cause you or your children." This should absolve them of any future claims of liability from their parishioners which appears to have been the mission, after all.

Survivors of sexual abuse by clergy finally bring civil action when they realize that their church is unwilling to give them what they deserve: a chance to tell their story, an acknowledgement of what was done to them, assurance that this person will not ever again be in a position to harm others, and financial compensation for their counseling expenses. But I have never met a survivor of clergy abuse who really wanted to sue their church.

As the bishops gathered in Dallas in 2002, the most significant thing that happened there were the testimonies delivered by survivors. Some bishops were transformed by listening to survivors. Every bishop had to listen, to be in that place of sharing the victims' suffering, and then to look, not to lawyers, but to the Gospel for direction.

Fr. Cozzens is asking the important questions, the systemic questions, not just "how do we clean up this mess?" but "how did we get in this mess in the first place?" For one thing, this question moves beyond the immediate crisis of disclosures of sexual abuse of children and includes sexual abuse of adults also. The issue is not even about sex *per se* but about the exploitation of vulnerability, regardless of the age of the victim. Slowly the reality of adult women and some men whose pastoral relationships have been violated by priests are coming to the fore. This will be the next wave of the tsunami to hit the church.

What seems to be missing is a fundamental understanding of the nature of the problem and the ethics at stake. It is a violation of professional ethics for any person in a ministerial role of leadership or ministerial counseling (clergy or lay) to engage in sexual contact or sexualized behavior with a congregant, client, employee, student, etc. (adult, teen, or child) within the professional (ministerial or supervisory) relationship.

Why is it wrong for a minister to be sexual with someone whom he/she serves or supervises? It is wrong because sexual activity *in this context* is exploitative and abusive.

> *It is a violation of role.* The ministerial relationship presupposes certain role expectations. The minister/counselor is expected to make available certain resources, talents, knowledge, and expertise which will serve the best interest of the congregant, client, staff member, student intern, etc. Sexual contact is not part of the ministerial, professional role.

> *It is a misuse of authority and power.* The role of minister/counselor carries with it authority and power and the attendant responsibility to use this power to benefit the people who call upon the minister/counselor for service. This power can easily be misused, as is the case when a minister/counselor uses (intentionally or unintentionally) his/her authority to initiate or pursue sexual contact with a congregant, client, etc. Even if it is the congregant who sexualizes the relationship, it is still the minister/counselor's responsibility to maintain the boundaries of the ministerial relationship and not pursue a sexual relationship.

> *It is taking advantage of vulnerability.* The congregant, client, employee, student intern, etc. is by definition vulnerable to the minister/counselor, i.e., in multiple ways, she/he has fewer resources and less power than the minister/counselor. When the minister/counselor takes advantage of this vulnerability to gain sexual access to her/him, the minister/counselor violates the mandate to protect the vulnerable from harm. The protection of the vulnerable is a practice which derives from the Jewish and Christian traditions of a hospitality code.

> *It is an absence of meaningful consent.* Meaningful consent to sexual activity requires a context of not only choice but mutuality and equality; hence meaningful consent requires the absence of fear or the most subtle coercion. There is always an imbalance of power and thus inequality between the person in the ministerial role and those whom

he/she serves or supervises. Even in the relationship between two persons who see themselves as "consenting adults," the difference in role precludes the possibility of meaningful consent.

The proposed revisions to the Roman Catholic Bishops' Dallas Policy on the sexual abuse of children hold some interesting revelations. The Bishops directly tied the definition of sexual abuse to a moral standard based on the 6th Commandment in Hebrew scripture. "You shall not commit adultery." If this is the basis of their ethical understanding of sexual abuse, then no wonder the perception persists that the bishops simply don't "get it." The average layperson would rightly ask, "I thought adultery was about adults having sex with someone they are not married to. What does sexual abuse of kids have to do with adultery?"

The fundamental ethical question is "Why is it wrong for an adult to be sexual with a child or teen?" The answer is not rocket science. It is a betrayal of trust, a misuse of adult authority, the taking advantage of a child's vulnerability, and sexual activity in the absence of meaningful consent. When you add to this the fact of a priest being sexual with a child, it is also a betrayal of the role of the pastor. Our job as clergy is to nurture the flock, protect them when they are vulnerable, empower them in their lives–especially children and youth. Our people assume they can trust us not to harm them–because we are clergy. Sexual abuse betrays that trust.

In other words, sexual abuse harms the child or teen. It is a sin to cause this harm. In Christian scripture, Jesus is very clear: "It would be better for you if a millstone were hung around your neck and you were thrown into the sea than for you to cause one of these little ones to stumble," (Luke 17:2). The bishops got the wrong commandment. Instead of the 6th, they should have gone to the 7th: "You shall not steal." To steal is to take something that doesn't belong to you. To sexually abuse a child is to steal their innocence and their future, often with profound and tragic consequences.

When an acknowledged pedophile priest can say that he didn't see what was wrong with his behavior with a child since he was taught not to have sex with adult women, we can begin to see the inadequacy of this ethical analysis. The sexual abuse of a child or teen is about the misuse of power by the adult. It is about theft: taking advantage of a child's naivete, stealing his or her future.

The Roman Catholic Bishops will never be able to move forward and restore credibility to the church and the priesthood unless they can get their commandments right. They should be worrying about the theft of their children, not about some abstraction of adultery.

Finally, this is not about celibacy or scape-goating gay priests. It is about boundaries, power, and vulnerability. It is about training and screening. And it is about the transparency of accountability and accountability to the people of the parishes, not just the hierarchy. The media did not create this problem. Protestants did not create this problem. A minority of the clergy created this problem and the hierarchy all too often turned a blind eye or aided and abetted abusing priests with little or no thought to the well-being of the children.

The only way through the valley of the shadow of death is *through* the valley of the shadow of death. I realize that some bishops are on this journey, thanks be to God. But others must join. From a place of confession and penance, asking for help, willing to work for the hard answers, not the easy ones.

The church's credibility *can* be restored, depending on how it responds to this crisis. The people don't expect perfection from their clergy. But when we fall short, they should expect confession, acknowledgement of responsibility, repentance, and protection by the powers that be.

Judy Beals, a Boston activist working for many years to address sexual abuse, made these comments in an editorial following the disclosure of the Boston crisis:

> The turning point in every social justice movement occurs when the authentic leadership of survivors is met with the genuine commitments of our most powerful social institutions. The result, inevitably, is the strengthening of existing systems that work and the continual development of new innovations, protections, and partnerships that we have yet to even imagine. If there is any silver lining to the recent tragic events, it is the opportunity to channel public outrage into lasting structures and commitments that will rid society of sexual violence. If we fail to do this, the shame is ours. (Beals, 2002)

Beals is correct in her assessment. We, as members and leaders of our churches, have an opportunity to change the church–not only to address this current crisis but also to prevent its reoccurrence in the future.

REFERENCE

Beals, Judith, "Action on Sexual Violence," *The Boston Globe*, April 1, 2002.

Response to Fr. Donald B. Cozzens

Howard J. Hubbard

SUMMARY. This essay is a direct response by Bishop Hubbard, the Roman Catholic Diocese of Albany, New York, to the keynote by Fr. Donald B. Cozzens. In it he basically supports Fr. Cozzens comments and uses his experience in the Diocese of Albany to illustrate his concerns about response to sexual abuse by priests. *[Article copies available for a fee from The Haworth Document Delivery Service: 1-800-HAWORTH. E-mail address: <docdelivery@haworthpress.com> Website: <http://www.HaworthPress.com> © 2003 by The Haworth Press, Inc. All rights reserved.]*

KEYWORDS. Clergy sexual abuse, Fr. Donald B. Cozzens, Roman Catholic sex abuse crisis, Diocese of Albany

I am grateful to Fr. Donald Cozzens for his insightful and challenging presentation, and for the many and varied ways he continues to raise a prophetic voice in our church and society. I read and quote him frequently. Certainly, there is much in Fr. Cozzens' presentation I would like to affirm and reecho.

I agree wholeheartedly that our faith community has suffered a serious and scandalous wound and we have yet to understand fully its true nature, depth and scope. There is the two-fold scandal of the breach of sacred trust by individual priests and the way bishops like myself have

---

[Haworth co-indexing entry note]: "Response to Fr. Donald B. Cozzens." Hubbard, Howard J. Co-published simultaneously in *Journal of Religion & Abuse* (The Haworth Pastoral Press, an imprint of The Haworth Press, Inc.) Vol. 5, No. 3, 2003, pp. 59-65; and: *Sexual Abuse in the Catholic Church: Trusting the Clergy?* (ed: Marie M. Fortune, and W. Merle Longwood) The Haworth Pastoral Press, an imprint of The Haworth Press, Inc., 2003, pp. 59-65. Single or multiple copies of this article are available for a fee from The Haworth Document Delivery Service [1-800-HAWORTH, 9:00 a.m. - 5:00 p.m. (EST). E-mail address: docdelivery@haworthpress.com].

mishandled such misconduct, because of ignorance, fear or the misguided attempt to protect the church from scandal. Indeed, as Fr. Cozzens has noted, this moral ineptitude in giving greater priority to the church's image than to the protection of children has now become the scandal.

I applaud and join Fr. Cozzens' call for the laity to step up and assume their birthright as full, adult members and leaders in our faith communities. This has been a constant theme through my episcopacy and, if there is a ray of light to emerge from this tragedy, I hope it will be an even more informed and active laity.

Such a development should result in a willingness to address seriously and constructively the important ecclesial issues Fr. Cozzens addressed in his presentation: the nature of authority in the church, the role of hierarchy and the discipline of celibacy. I am confident that such a candid discussion would bear rich fruit and be guided by the Spirit.

I pray further that this greater involvement on the part of laity will not only be related to this misconduct scandal itself, but also be about how to make our faith communities the dynamic and caring wellsprings of spirituality, love, justice and service God intends them to be.

I would like to focus my response on some of the complexities involved in translating to reality the vision that Fr. Cozzens has articulated.

For example, I concur with Father Cozzens' call for transparency and accountability about the number of perpetrators, victims and costs associated with the scandal. Here I believe is where the National Review Board, chaired by former Oklahoma Governor Frank Keating, can make an enormous contribution by ascertaining these figures, and any diocesan bishop who does not comply should be subject to censure or removal.

The Albany Diocese embraces the principles of transparency articulated in the Charter. Since Dallas our policy has been and continues to be the following: public identification of priests who have been removed or suspended; public reporting on the aggregate dollar value of settlements reached; public reporting on the costs of assessment and treatment of clergy offenders, counseling for victims and their family members, legal and consultant fees; and public reporting on all of the programs in place to prevent sexual abuse from recurring and to create safe environments for children. In conjunction with the study to be conducted this spring by the National Review Board, our Diocese is committed to releasing the cost figures associated with this issue.

But there are some practical challenges that must be addressed. Some still insist that the church is hiding information when, for instance, we decline to identify individuals under investigation who are the subject of yet unsubstantiated allegations, or when we decline to reveal information shared by victims in confidential meetings. The goal of transparency clearly is not to punish the innocent, traumatize victims or invade properly confidential meetings. The goal, as we see it, is to protect the community against abusers and give the laity and the public access to information on–and therefore greater control over–the church's management of these matters.

In the Albany Diocese, we've taken the step of reviewing all allegations with the Diocesan Review Board (composed of 9 members, 7 of whom are laity, not in the employ of the Diocese). If an accused priest is believed to pose an imminent threat to the community or if the information provided by our investigator leads to the assessment there are reasonable grounds to believe the abuse may have occurred, the priest is placed on administrative leave and that action is made known publicly. In addition, we will send to the board for review all proposed settlements with victims to ensure that they are fair and just to all parties. All of this comports with the church's commitment to transparency.

With regard to accountability, I believe the National Review Board can make an enormous contribution by commissioning scientific research on the data it compiles. Catholics and other members of the public have raised legitimate questions about the underlying causes of sexual abuse by clergy. These questions deserve answers based on careful research, not anecdotal evidence or preconceived assumptions. In his presentation, for example, Fr. Cozzens hypothesizes that the problem of the sexual abuse of children is higher among priests. A well researched study would help to determine if this assertion is factually true–but at the moment that remains speculative. Hence, I welcome the results of studies such as that of the John Jay School of Criminal Justice that the National Review Board has already commissioned.

The media's coverage of the scandal is also marked by complexity. On the one hand, the media are to be credited for exposing the scandal and for pursuing it persistently. On the other hand, as Archbishop Flynn pointed out in his presentation, media accounts often fail to provide context about where and when the problem occurred, how it was handled and what has been done or is being done to address it. Further, as Peter Steinfels of the *New York Times* observes, many in the media consistently cite authorities or experts who have an advocacy position on this issue, but fail to offer the spectrum of opinions on a very complex subject (Steinfels, 2002, pp. 9-11).

More specifically, our diocese has been making a concerted effort to respond to victims by hiring a victim's assistance coordinator and an investigator, expanding the membership of our diocesan review board, developing training programs for parish staff and volunteers, and arranging for criminal background checks for employees and volunteers. These efforts seek to build upon some long standing policies and procedures relative to the screening and education of our clergy and programs for safe environments. Yet, most media attention continues to focus on allegations 20, 30, and 40 years old and the legal action surrounding them. The church's constructive response to victims is a vastly under-reported story.

Another complexity involves the question about the church's legal responsibility, and how it should participate in the process of determining the nature and extent of its liability. As Mark Sargent, the Dean of the Villanova University School of Law observed in a June 2002 issue of *Commonweal*, legal responsibility must be disentangled from moral responsibility, because although certainly related, they are not coextensive. Sargent says, "The church's institutional and moral responsibility for the creation and perpetuation of this scandal is obvious . . . the integrity of the church, and particularly of the hierarchy, will be measured by its willingness to respond to this profound moral crisis . . . Acceptance of that moral responsibility, however, does not mean that every church institution must always accept the level of legal responsibility as defined by every plaintiff's lawyer" (Sargent, 2002, pp. 13-15).

We in the Diocese of Albany recognize and fully accept our moral responsibility to right the wrongs suffered by victims of clergy sexual abuse, but this does not mean that we naively accept the validity of every plaintiff attorney's claim about the abuse itself and its attendant circumstances, how a church institution or an individual within the church were complicit in the abuse or negligent in dealing with it, and what level of compensatory and punitive damage is justified until such assertions are subject to thorough scrutiny. To take this posture is not to deny that there was sexual abuse by clergy, but simply to recognize that not every claim is necessarily meritorious, or at least meritorious to the extent asserted, and that the church may be justified in mediating or, if necessary, litigating some claims.

There are many other important issues involving lawsuits stemming from clergy sexual abuse, which time does not permit me to address, and about which, quite frankly, there are no facile solutions. For example, should current knowledge of "best practices" necessarily be the standard for determining legal liability for decisions made 20 or 30 years ago; or if liability is conceded, how does one assess the monetary compensation? Even among professionals in the field there is plenty of room for reasonable disagreement about how much even a just claim is worth.

In this latter regard, Father Cozzens states that "we must put the spiritual and personal welfare of those wounded ahead of everything else, including the welfare of our respective institutions." Certainly, care for victims must be a priority for the church. But does that mean that leaders of a Diocese must be willing to sacrifice the welfare of the church—and all of the spiritual, academic, health care and social programs provided by the church in society? Bringing financial or institutional ruin to the church, even in a well intentioned attempt to right the wrongs, would deprive Catholics and the broader society of the church's spiritual leadership and its humanitarian, health-care, educational and social services. What about the other wounded populations we serve? Do we abandon our work with children with AIDS, our advocacy programs for the developmentally disabled, our outreach programs for the victims of domestic violence, our housing programs for the homeless, etc.? I would note also that the resources of the Church are far more limited than many may suspect.

What is needed, then, I believe, is practical guidance and counsel to church leaders in striking the appropriate balance: How much of our resources should properly be devoted to providing a compassionate and comprehensive response to the crisis, including compensation to victims, and how much to continuing to support all of the other important church programs that serve society in an uncertain economic climate characterized by increasing human needs, reduced philanthropic giving and glaring budget deficit at the local, state, and federal levels?

Similarly, Father Cozzens suggests that until the church deals constructively with the misconduct scandal, its leaders are not in a position to exercise moral and spiritual leadership in our church and society. He notes people are saying to us, "Physician heal thyself before you speak of healing and salvation."

I agree that only by constructive action with regard to the sexual misconduct issue can church leaders re-earn the trust of Catholics and the public. In the meantime, however, I believe for the church to go silent, to suspend its spiritual and moral leadership in other realms—as a voice against the war with Iraq, for example, or as a champion for the poor in the face of the current government budget deficits—would be wrong, and ultimately destructive to the mission of the Church; not a victory over sexual abuse but a victory for all who would eliminate spiritual, moral, and ethical perspectives from the public square.

Here, again, I would suggest a balanced approach is necessary. The church must re-earn its position of trust, in part, by continuing to be a voice of morality, hope and faith. Church leaders face the practical problem of finding the right balance. I would welcome practical suggestions on how bishops and others in our church might continue to assert the proper level of spiritual leadership while recognizing the natural skepticism/cynicism of some audiences due to the scandal.

A final complexity I would cite is the issue of treatment for victims. Much to the shame of the church, we too long denied or minimized the needs of victims and their families. This failure to reach out to those abused and to provide psychological, pastoral and spiritual care led to disastrous consequences for many victims including, as I can attest to from firsthand interaction with victims: free floating anger, guilt, low self-esteem, alcohol and substance abuse, the loss of motivation for education or career advancement, the inability to form trusting, intimate relationships, and the loss of faith.

Fortunately, most church authorities now recognize the need to provide professional and pastoral assistance to victims/survivors, and many have or are benefiting from such outreach. The guilt or stigma associated with having been abused is gradually being removed and victims are reclaiming broken dreams and shattered lives. This is certainly a great blessing and both the press and survivor groups deserve much of the credit.

Because of sad past experiences, however, and the lack of trust in authority figures, which is an understandable consequence of child sexual abuse, there has often developed an adversarial relationship between victim/survivor groups and church leadership, which at times makes a pastoral response on the part of the church difficult, if not impossible. I hope, then, that prospectively, ways can be found for church leaders and members of victims' groups to work more cooperatively and collaboratively in the healing process. The concept of restorative justice as the foundation for a process of healing and reconciliation may be an area where we can find common ground.

In conclusion, in raising these issues of complexities, I am not trying to minimize the terrible harm that has been done by clergy sexual abuse, to absolve the church of its responsibility, to deflect criticism or, God forbid, to suggest I have the answers. Rather I am merely trying to point out that there are multiple facets to this issue which must be assessed and weighed carefully in developing and implementing appropriate responses. Hopefully, through the type of presentations and respectful dialog that appears here, we can find suitable mechanisms and solutions that will genuinely contribute to healing for victims and their families, to the protection of our most precious heritage, our youth, and to reform and renewal within the church.

REFERENCES

Sargent, Mark, "Should the Church Defend Itself in Court," *Commonweal*, Vol. CXXIX, No. 12 (June 14, 2002).

Steinfels, Peter, "Abused by the Media," *London Tablet*, (September 14, 2002).

The Sexual Abuse Crisis–
Issues We Still Have to Face:
Response to Fr. Donald B. Cozzens

Carolyn Moore Newberger

SUMMARY. This essay is a direct response to Fr. Donald Cozzens' keynote at the Symposium "Trusting the Clergy: The churches and communities come to grips with sexual misconduct." It focuses on the issues we still have to face concerning sexual abuse in the Catholic Church, which are: How do we know what the truth is when there are sexual abuse allegations; and how do we protect children from such abuse? *[Article copies available for a fee from The Haworth Document Delivery Service: 1-800-HAWORTH. E-mail address: <docdelivery@haworthpress.com> Web site: <http://www.HaworthPress.com> © 2003 by The Haworth Press, Inc. All rights reserved.]*

KEYWORDS. Clergy sexual abuse, Roman Catholic sex abuse crisis

The Catholic Church in America is not going to go away. I hope and expect that it will continue as a vibrant force in people's lives, and as a safe haven in all the many ways that it has the potential to offer. What this means is that we are still going to have children in our churches and

[Haworth co-indexing entry note]: "The Sexual Abuse Crisis–Issues We Still Have to Face: Response to Fr. Donald B. Cozzens." Newberger, Carolyn Moore. Co-published simultaneously in *Journal of Religion & Abuse* (The Haworth Pastoral Press, an imprint of The Haworth Press, Inc.) Vol. 5, No. 3, 2003, pp. 67-74; and: *Sexual Abuse in the Catholic Church: Trusting the Clergy?* (ed: Marie M. Fortune, and W. Merle Longwood) The Haworth Pastoral Press, an imprint of The Haworth Press, Inc., 2003, pp. 67-74. Single or multiple copies of this article are available for a fee from The Haworth Document Delivery Service [1-800-HAWORTH, 9:00 a.m. - 5:00 p.m. (EST). E-mail address: docdelivery@haworthpress.com].

http://www.haworthpress.com/web/JORA
© 2003 by The Haworth Press, Inc. All rights reserved.
Digital Object Identifier: 10.1300/J154v05n03_10

those children are still going to come under the care of our leaders. We need to think urgently about how to protect the children who will come under our care in the future.

I indicated in my previous essay how difficult it is to recognize abusers. The reality is that it is very difficult to know whether someone is what he seems (Salter, 2003, p. 196). I would like to reflect on the implications of that reality as we think about some of the policies articulated in the "Charter for the Protection of Children and Young People" that were discussed by Archbishop Flynn (United State Conference of Catholic Bishops, 2002). I would like to point to two of the Articles in which I see embedded profound issues that we still have to face, and to use these issues as a springboard for knowledge and awareness that you may be able to factor into your thinking and actions in the months and years ahead.

Article 2 states that "Dioceses/eparchies will have mechanisms in place to respond promptly to any allegation where there is reason to believe that sexual abuse of a minor has occurred." The issue is, what is "reason to believe"? Who determines that there is "reason to believe"? Let me tell you about a conversation I had with a priest. He described a situation where two children recently came forward independently with credible allegations about sexual activity with a priest. The accused priest, he said, is also very credible in his denial of those allegations. This very concerned priest was in a quandary about who was telling the truth.

The reality is that in most situations where allegations of sexual abuse occur, there is a very high degree of ambiguity. These cases are rarely clear. In order to achieve greater clarity, you need to know about how children disclose, and about how people who abuse children operate. For example, the Reverend Donald Cozzens in his essay described a colleague, a professor of moral theology, who was determined to have sex with a male teen-age student. This professor had a great cover for his obsessions. He chose an arena in which he was unlikely to be suspect. It is important to recognize that people who abuse children will construct a life, and lead a double life, in which they present as nice people (De Becker, 1997). They do good deeds, they say the right things, they are apparently sincere believers, and they may actually be sincere believers. But they are still people who prey on children. They are still a danger to children.

When you are trying to determine which of the conflicting stories, the alleged victim's or the alleged perpetrator's, you have the greatest "reason to believe," you must understand that a priest who has the appearance of piety, who demonstrates good deeds reflecting care and concern, who reflects all the qualities that you consider valuable in a priest, may not believe any of it. Or, he may believe some of it, but that does not mean that he is not abusing children. I am sure we all know of situations where people in the community cannot believe that a particular scoutmaster, teacher, or cleric could have possibly done this to children. But very often being the proverbial pillar of the community is one of the ways that a person gets away with abuse. It is one of the ways that he gains parents' trust and access to their children, and seduces children unsuspectingly into sexual behavior.

To complicate judgment further, when children disclose sexual abuse, they often disclose in a way that is not very believable or straightforward (Sorenson & Snow, 1991). First, children are often afraid to disclose. Studies of college students and adults reveal that those who had been sexually abused in their childhoods rarely told someone about it (Sauzier, 1989). I do not doubt that children today, with greater education and awareness, are more likely to disclose than were children in the past. Yet even so, there is reason to believe that many abused children still do not disclose. Those who do disclose often wait months or years before telling someone. Why? They don't disclose because they feel that they won't be believed, that it will bring trouble to their families, because they are afraid they or someone else will be harmed if they tell. They may believe that what is happening is their fault; they may be ashamed or feel stigmatized. This is especially the case with boys, who worry particularly about their sexuality and adequacy in the eyes of other children (Black & De Blassie, 1993; Finkelhor & Brown, 1985).

Children also might not disclose because someone they fear and/or respect has told them that this is a secret. Sometimes children love their abusers, and don't want to get them into trouble or lose the love and attention that person gives to them. Don't forget that people who abuse children are manipulative. They manipulate people around them into believing that they are upstanding citizens, and they manipulate children into these fears and feelings so that the children will maintain the secrecy of the abuse (Singer, Hussey, & Strom, 1992).

When children do disclose, the majority don't just come out and tell their story (Sorenson & Snow, 1991). Sometimes abuse is revealed directly. Teenagers are more likely to tell someone directly than are younger children. More typically, sexual abuse in revealed indirectly or piecemeal. I have conducted a research study that looked at children's disclosures. The abuse of one child in the study was discovered after a playmate reported to her mother that her friend was rubbing the Ken and Barbie dolls together in a way that made the little girl uncomfortable. That child's mother reported this to the abused child's mother, who called protective services after questioning her daughter. The abuser was identified and confessed.

Sexual abuse can also be discovered in other ways. For example, an adult might walk in on a child being abused. A pediatrician might discover that the patient's vaginal complaints are caused by chlamydia. When children do tell, however, they often tell over time, with pieces of their experience emerging over days, weeks, or months. Sometimes children will disclose sexual abuse and then insist that what they said isn't true. Although people may interpret retractions as proof that the abuse didn't happen, it is far more likely for children to retract because they see that people get upset and angry, sometimes at them, that they may not be believed, that it brings trouble to the family, and that it brings pain to the people that love them. The child may feel that he or she has done something wrong, and attempt to undo the damage by insisting that it didn't really happen, or that only some of it happened, or that it really happened to someone else. In the pain and confusion that accompanies disclosure, a child may yearn to return to the more stable pre-disclosure state, even at the expense of continuing abuse. Significantly, the majority of children who say they were mistaken after they have disclosed sexual abuse eventually reaffirm that they had been abused (Bradley & Woods, 1996; Sorenson & Snow, 1991).

As you can see, the ways children disclose do not always lend themselves intuitively to "reason to believe." Unless you know how children disclose, you are likely to dismiss many of their disclosures as not believable. Sometimes the question you have to ask yourself is, "Why would a child lie to get into trouble?" We know why a perpetrator would lie to get out of trouble. Not infrequently, greater clarity can be achieved in these ambiguous situations when you ask, "Who has the greatest motive to lie?"

Usually the person with the greatest motive to lie is someone who is trying to cover something bad that he or she has done. Children can also lie. In cases of clergy abuse, however, I don't think it is very likely, because I cannot think of many motives for a child to lie. As a consequence, I believe that every allegation must be approached as reasonable and appropriately pursued. And, for the good of the child and his or her family, take the stance that the child is to be believed, not a skeptical or doubting attitude.

Archbishop Flynn also made reference to Article 5 in the "Charter for the Protection of Children and Young People." Within this article is a statement that an allegation of sexual abuse of a minor by a priest or deacon will initiate "a preliminary investigation, in harmony with canon law." "If this investigation so indicates," further steps will be taken, including reporting the priest or deacon to civil authorities, relieving the alleged offender of his ministerial duties, and possibly requesting medical and psychological evaluation. The unanswered question is, what is "sufficient evidence" to indicate "further steps"? You may never acquire sufficient evidence. Are you going to let that priest continue in his pastoral duties while you gather more evidence, or decide that insufficient evidence is a reason not to take further action? I would argue that in order to protect children, the church and clergy have to be willing to make hard choices, between assuring that children are protected and trusting your brethren.

In the face of a suspicion or allegation of sexual abuse by a priest, one must act. Two principal choices and consequent courses of action may be taken: to choose to believe that the priest could not have abused and that the allegation is false; or to choose to believe that the priest may have abused and that the allegation is credible. Each course of action could be correct, but each choice also contains the possibility that it is incorrect. In the face of ambiguity where a choice must be made, ask yourself, which is the more tolerable error. Is the more tolerable error to respond as though the priest has not abused, when in fact he has, with the risk that a child or children may continue to be molested? Or is the more tolerable error to respond as though the priest may have abused, with the risk that an innocent man will suffer emotionally and professionally from that misjudgment?

The consequences of both errors are profound. Some situations are clearer than others and carry less risk of error. Other situations, perhaps most, are highly ambiguous and the risk of error is high. Under these circumstances, I would argue that the second error is the more tolerable. The costs to children both of continued abuse and of not being believed and protected are catastrophic. The costs to priests of being falsely accused are also high, but they are not children. They have greater resources and resiliency with which to understand and to recover from that blow.

It is also important to remember that these are preliminary rather than permanent decisions. Once the church accepts that an allegation must be acted upon, according to Article 4, the case is referred to the civil authorities. I believe that if priests are trained to understand the difficult choices that must be made, and why allegations much be presumed credible in ambiguous situations, they will be able to accept the sacrifices an innocently accused priest must bear for the good of the community and the greater protection of children.

Now I would like to discuss what we can do to protect the children who are with us now and in the future. As parents, we can protect our children by being present at their activities where they might have contact with adults (Salter, 2003, pp. 223-226).

Institutions such as Boy Scouts of America have comprehensive policies for protecting children (Boy Scouts of America, 2001). Boy Scouts is a high-risk environment, just as a church is a high-risk environment, and their policies include screening practices for leadership selection, youth protection training for all leaders and volunteers, sexual abuse prevention education for their scouts, and the requirement that no scout leader can be alone with a child. These policies protect not only children, but also those who work with children. Such a careful and comprehensive policy is important for the church as well. You have to assume that anyone with access to children, along with the potential for privacy and secrecy, can prey on children. Don't allow the privacy. Don't provide the opportunities. If parents are involved routinely in activities that include children, both the children and the church will be better protected (Salter, ibid.).

To conclude, I would like to raise a different issue. As we have discussed, predators can be very deceptive. One of the issues I did not discuss is how difficult it is to detect deception. Studies of deception reveal that no one is very good at knowing when somebody is lying. When people are practiced liars they can fool just about everybody, because that is their job. They are good at it and they are successful, or they would not be able to abuse children. The most skilled detectors, such as secret service agents and police, under the best of circumstances, correctly detect deception about sixty percent of the time. For the rest of us the rate is random. In other words, we correctly detect deception about fifty percent of the time. And people who think they are really good at knowing when someone is lying are not any better than anyone else, they are just more insistent (Salter, 2003, p. 196).

Predators are deceptive. They are alluring. They can be kind and considerate. They may be pious. They may go out of their way to do good deeds. They flatter and seduce. Just as predators can lure you into believing that they are good priests, predators can also lure women into marriages where they and their children are abused. One of the tasks of professionals who work with these women is to help them get out of dangerous relationships safely.

The church and its priests are also acknowledged to be in a marriage. One might argue that, through their cleverness and allure, some predatory priests have seduced the church into that marriage. In response to your own crisis, the Dallas Charter recognizes that some priests may need to be severed from the clerical state. In other words, the Dallas Charter authorizes the divorce of a priest not only from priestly duties, but also sometimes from the priesthood itself, in the service of protecting children and of protecting the church.

I would urge you to think about the meaning of divorce. If the church can contain people who have misled them and harmed their own, so in marriages women can be misled and they and their children harmed. If severing a priest's sacramental ties to the church is permissible when he has committed such grievous betrayal and harm, so too should such severing of marriage be permissible. Under these circumstances, a woman needs and deserves the support and comfort of her church.

REFERENCES

Black, C.A., & De Blassie, R.R. "Sexual abuse in male children and adolescents: Indicators, effects and treatment." *Adolescence*, 1993. 28:123-133.

Boy Scouts of America. Youth Protection and Adult Leadership: Boy Scout and Cub Scout Leader Training Module, 2001 www.usscouts.org.

Bradley A.R., & Wood, J.M. "How do children tell? The disclosure process in child sexual abuse." *Child Abuse and Neglect*, 1996, 20:881-891.

Cromdie, W.J. Childhood abuse hurts the brain. *Harvard University Gazette*, May 22, 2003, page 1.

De Becker, G. *The Gift of Fear*, Boston: Little-Brown, 1997.

Finkelhor, D., & Brown, A. "The traumatic impact of child sexual abuse: A conceptualization." *American Journal of Orthopsychiatry*, 1985, 55:530-541.

Newberger C.M., & De Vos, E. Abuse and victimization: A life-span developmental perspective. *Am J Orthopsychiat*, 1988, 58:505-511.

Newberger C.M., & Newberger E.H. When the pedophile is a pediatrician. In: Burgess N.W., ed. *Sexual exploitation by health professionals*. New York, NY: Praeger, 1986, 99-106; reprinted in: Maney, A., ed. *Professionals and the sexual abuse of children: Public health approaches*. New York, NY: Praeger, 1988, 65-72.

Newberger, C.M., Gremy, I.M., Waternaux, C.M., & Newberger, E.H. Mothers of sexually abused children: Trauma and repair in longitudinal perspective. *American Journal of Orthopsychiatry*, 1993, 63:92-102.

Salter, A.C. *Predators, Pedophiles, Rapists, and Other Sex Offenders.* New York, NY: Basic Books, 2003.

Sauzier, M. "Disclosure of child sexual abuse: For better or worse." *Psychiatric Clinics of North America,* 1989, 12:455-469.

Singer, M.I., Hussey, D., & Strom, K.J. "Grooming the victim: An analysis of a perpetrator's seduction letter." *Child Abuse and Neglect,* 1992, 16:877-886.

Sorensen, T., & Snow, B. (1991). How children tell: The process of disclosure in child sexual abuse. Child Welfare, 70, 3-15.

United States Conference of Catholic Bishops, *Charter for the Protection of Children and Young People Revised Edition.* Washington, DC, 2002.

RESPONSES TO CLERGY SEXUAL ABUSE BY LOCAL LAY LEADERS REPRESENTING DIVERSE COMMUNITIES

A Response to Clergy Sexual Abuse: A Latina Perspective

Ladan Alomar

SUMMARY. This essay considers the problem of sexual abuse by clergy from a Latina perspective. *[Article copies available for a fee from The Haworth Document Delivery Service: 1-800-HAWORTH. E-mail address: <docdelivery@haworthpress.com> Website: <http://www.HaworthPress.com> © 2003 by The Haworth Press, Inc. All rights reserved.]*

KEYWORDS. Clergy sexual abuse, abuse by Roman Catholic clergy, Latino perspectives

[Haworth co-indexing entry note]: "A Response to Clergy Sexual Abuse: A Latina Perspective." Alomar, Ladan. Co-published simultaneously in *Journal of Religion & Abuse* (The Haworth Pastoral Press, an imprint of The Haworth Press, Inc.) Vol. 5, No. 3, 2003, pp. 75-77; and: *Sexual Abuse in the Catholic Church: Trusting the Clergy?* (ed: Marie M. Fortune, and W. Merle Longwood) The Haworth Pastoral Press, an imprint of The Haworth Press, Inc., 2003, pp. 75-77. Single or multiple copies of this article are available for a fee from The Haworth Document Delivery Service [1-800-HAWORTH, 9:00 a.m. - 5:00 p.m. (EST). E-mail address: docdelivery@haworthpress.com].

http://www.haworthpress.com/web/JORA
© 2003 by The Haworth Press, Inc. All rights reserved.

Digital Object Identifier: 10.1300/J154v05n03_11

I want to begin with a question: Who am I without my faith? Fate is the fundamental part of Latino culture and existence. For example, when I make an appointment with Mrs. Camacho and I tell her I'll see you tomorrow at nine, she responds, "Si Dios Quiere" (God willing). Her belief is, "Fate is in control of my destiny, rather than I am in control of my own destiny." There is a great difference between these two concepts, if you say I am in control or if you say God (fate) is in control.

Clergy sexual abuse has had a profound impact on the confidence in the integrity and honesty of the church officials. Our trust has been shattered. It is very sad that church officials have treated sexual assault as administrative problems or celibacy violations to be covered up by offering hush money and shifting priests from parish to parish. Rather than protecting the most vulnerable, the concern is to protect the church's image and by doing this, the message is that we support the abuser, rather than reject the abuser.

When a clergy member betrays moral authority and public trust, it is the ultimate betrayal. Last year Pope John Paul II acknowledged the crisis. That was a good thing, but far from enough. People want the truth and justice. People expect a new course of action to heal the wounds of victims and their families.

What is being done to resolve the problem? People need a concrete answer. The church should be more accountable to the legal authorities and the people it serves.

The culture of secrecy and cover-up is extremely disturbing. Finding solutions starts with the clergy being held accountable to the same standards as the congregations they serve. No professional group, such as doctors, lawyers and police, is good at policing itself. And for clergy it is even more difficult, because they were taught to forgive rather than punish.

Many times a point is made clearer by telling a story. And I believe in another life I was a storyteller.

Many, many years ago there was a village and in this village there was a wise man who, to the villagers, was the center of the village, the core of their existence and moral compass.

After many years the wise man died and all of the villagers came together to mourn and decide what to do, for he was the problem solver and always had the all the answers. They gathered together to identify another leader to guide them. The task was extremely difficult. The villagers agreed upon a new leader, a woman. She was kind, understanding and intelligent. They all voted in favor of her taking the role. All except two of the villagers were happy with the decision. These two met in private to talk. "What are we going to do about this? We have to think of something."

"I know," one said. "The next time we all gather in the village I am going to hide a small bird in my hands. I will ask her to tell me if the bird is alive or dead. If she says 'alive,' I will crush it in my hands. If she says 'dead,' I will set it free. There is no way she can answer correctly."

At the next assembly this individual anxiously waited for the woman to arrive. As he walked back and forth his hands loosened a bit and a small feather stuck out from his hands. The woman approached him and asked, "Do you have a small bird in your hands?" The individual replied, "Yes, but if you are so wise tell me if it is alive or dead?" She smiled and responded, "It is all up to you."

We are all angels with one wing, and we need each other to fly. There are many angels among us with a broken wing, the sexual abuse victims. They need our help and support to heal and to be able to fly again. The abuser also has a broken wing and needs our help, which is best served through justice and rehabilitation.

A Response to Clergy Sexual Abuse:
An African American Perspective

Anne M. Pope

SUMMARY. This article will reflect on the effects of priest sex abuse on the African American Community. *[Article copies available for a fee from The Haworth Document Delivery Service: 1-800-HAWORTH. E-mail address: <docdelivery@haworthpress.com> Website: <http://www.HaworthPress.com> © 2003 by The Haworth Press, Inc. All rights reserved.]*

KEYWORDS. Clergy sexual abuse, abuse by Roman Catholic clergy, African American perspectives

Let me begin by saying that the African American community and the Catholic community have enjoyed a tremendously popular working relationship here in the Albany (New York) area over the years. We have been involved in "twinning" with Catholic churches as the result of a relationship with Father Peter Young and Bishop Howard Hubbard and in many other efforts, such as combined worship services and advocacy on all fronts. Great strides have been made in creating community trust and a positive relationship. This relationship resulted in many of our students and our children attending parochial and private schools owned and sponsored by the Catholic Diocese. To my knowledge, there

[Haworth co-indexing entry note]: "A Response to Clergy Sexual Abuse: An African American Perspective." Pope, Anne M. Co-published simultaneously in *Journal of Religion & Abuse* (The Haworth Pastoral Press, an imprint of The Haworth Press, Inc.) Vol. 5, No. 3, 2003, pp. 79-85; and: *Sexual Abuse in the Catholic Church: Trusting the Clergy?* (ed: Marie M. Fortune, and W. Merle Longwood) The Haworth Pastoral Press, an imprint of The Haworth Press, Inc., 2003, pp. 79-85. Single or multiple copies of this article are available for a fee from The Haworth Document Delivery Service [1-800-HAWORTH, 9:00 a.m. - 5:00 p.m. (EST). E-mail address: docdelivery@haworthpress.com].

has never been a serious problem of abuse in any form. Overall, it has been very meaningful and beneficial for the future of our youth.

To illustrate the relationship, I will share the story of my son and daughter who both graduated from private Catholic schools. In 1970, my two children, Harold and Gwen, and I were vacationing in my home town of Shubuta in Southeast Mississippi when my son, Harold, asked in a matter of fact way, "Ma, would you find me a new school when we get back?" At the time, he was attending Giffen Elementary School, which was right across the street from where we lived. I said "yes," knowing that I would do anything I needed to do to ensure that my children got the best education money could buy, even if it meant getting a second job. He expressed a desire to attend St. John's Roman Catholic School, which was a block and a half away from where we lived.

I immediately began to put the wheels in motion to see if I could get him into St. John's. I succeeded, and Harold started school at St. John's Roman Catholic school that September. He went to school with glee every day and even became an altar boy, serving with Father Peter Young and then Father Howard Hubbard. (Little did he know that he was serving with a soon-to-be famous bishop.)

He served proudly, getting up early in the morning to serve 7:00 o'clock mass. He was an active Baptist, but he was proud of his role as an altar boy and proud to be attending a Catholic school.

He graduated from St. John's in the 6th grade and went into the 7th grade. He then asked me, with no thought of the cost associated with it, if he could go to Christian Brothers Academy, another Catholic school. He enrolled, he attended and he did well. He was on the honor roll, in the Wanesbara Rifle Club and all of those things that make for a well-rounded education. He was a high jump celebrity. He stayed after school to engage in activities almost every night. He did his homework at school, and one of the priests taught him to play backgammon, which became his favorite game. CBA became his home away from home, as he loved his school. He developed a great sense of pride; he became a young man of dignity, distinction and honor.

He graduated from college and went into the military, married and had two sons. When he was making a career transition, shifting from military to civilian life, he sent his oldest son, Courtney, to live with me to attend Christian Brothers Academy. Neither he nor his son had any problems with Catholic school. Neither did his sister, Gwen, who attended both Marylrose Academy, now Holy Names Academy, and graduated from Mercy High School. She, too, went on to college and got a Masters Degree. Her first job was working for Catholic Maternity Services (CMS).

She enjoyed working with the young pregnant girls, helping them create a life for themselves. She currently serves on the Advisory Board for CMS. She keeps in contact with and adores Sister Maureen Joyce and Father Peter Young as well as Bishop Hubbard.

Throughout the years, we have had the utmost respect for the Catholic Diocese, the Catholic Church, and Catholic schools. We continue to remain involved in a variety of ways with the Catholic church or organizations that support these schools.

I am saddened to note that the church is now faced with this terrible dilemma, that those who have been trusted are now found to be not trustworthy. The main word, the operative word on the issue of sex abuse and the clergy, is *TRUST*.

As we read about the various incidents of clergy abuse, what we find more than anything else is the *faith* and *trust* the abused children and their parents and/or families had in the abuser. They welcomed these priests into their families and opened the doors of their lives and deepest secrets to them, only to be deceived by them.

In my community and in my culture, members of the clergy are held in high esteem. They are considered to be next to God. And since they ascribe to the notion that they have been called out from the called out, they are put on pedestals and are given a respect that is second only to the respect that we give God. Since they are the earthly vessels through which we are able to see and communicate with God in-person, this gives them another dimension of communication and interaction.

As an example of how clergy people are well-respected, in my culture it is a tradition for families to invite preachers to their homes for dinner after church. A feast is prepared fit for a king.

Two or three meats, four or five vegetables, two or three starches and tons of desserts of all kinds, too numerous to count–cakes, pies, puddings, ice creams of all flavors–coffee, kool-aid, iced tea, water; everything but wine is served. People bring out the best china, silverware and crystal. They would float a loan in order to set this table.

Friends of mine, especially male friends, often joke today about the preacher coming for dinner in their house and eating up everything! Including all the good parts of the chicken, leaving them nothing but the boney parts.

A second example is that when we were growing up the *law* of the land was that we were not allowed to go to the movies on Sunday. One Sunday after church, a group of us went to the movies and showed up late for the Baptist Training Union. When we arrived at church, our pastor, Rev. Pierce, called us into the choir stand and chastised us. I was so hurt I cried all the way home. I couldn't imagine how he knew. My mother opened the door and said "I knew it would be handled." I wondered how she knew that he had spoken to us. Then I realized she knew because it was she who had turned us in to the pastor. She trusted him to do her disciplining. Needless to say, we never went to the movies again on Sunday. If we did, we never let mama nor the pastor know we went. As I mentioned earlier, the preacher was next to God. He was trusted and revered. Throughout history, even people who are not religious have had a profound sense of trust for members of the clergy. It was as if there was something supernatural or mysterious surrounding them. We have a great sense of dedication to the "Men of the Cloth."

African Americans in particular have an unfaltering, unflagging respect and blind loyalty to "preachers." The same can be said about the kind of respect we have for "priests." I do not know of anyone who does not respect "priests," especially Catholic priests, and nuns as well. That respect can be verified by how many of us send our children to Catholic schools. We trust and believe that Catholic schools provide better educational opportunities for our children, and because of the religious education they receive there, we know our kids will be better citizens.

It is sad that we have come to this moment in society when the trust that individuals have in *any* community has been eroded and church members have to look askance at the people whom God has entrusted with lives and souls to lead us to him. I believe that it is a sin for anyone who has garnered the respect of people to betray their trust. It is criminal, and it has to be addressed and treated as such.

Victims of sex abuse by priests have had their trust betrayed, their bodies violated and their minds messed up. It is not just a violation of human rights, it is a criminal act, and it is my feeling and belief that these priests should be dealt with as any other criminal. By not treating them as criminals as other citizens are treated and punished, it appears to the abused that they are institutionally covered and protected from consequences.

It also appears as if the abused and their families are being intimidated by the corporate entity of the church. Most of the victims have little or no means of fighting back. It leaves them with the feeling "You can't fight City Hall." I am certain that in their training priests are taught how to deal appropriately with those they counsel. I am sure they are enjoined to be mindful of how they can trample on people's feelings, how they can use their influence and how fragile people are. They *are* privileged people. They are people of authority. Because they are privileged people, they are to be mindful of how they use their privileges.

Those of us in leadership roles know the dangers of abusing power. We know that "absolute power corrupts absolutely" and because we believe, as the scriptures teach, "to whom much is given–much is required," we submit ourselves to the will of God and ask him to *lead* and *guide* us, that we will never harm anyone, especially the young.

The scripture also teaches us that we are not to harm our young–not one hair on their heads–that it would be "better if a millstone were hung around your neck" (Luke 17:2).

In a May 2002 article of *BlackLight online*, entitled "Catholic Sex Scandal Comes to Black America," Sidney Brinkley states that since the current sex abuse scandal in the Catholic Church surfaced in January the cast of characters–both perpetrator and victim–has been decidedly white. But that changed on Monday, May 13, when Dontee Stokes shot Rev. Maurice Blackwell–once one of the most prominent African Americans in the Catholic Church–for an alleged sexual molestation that took place nine years earlier.

Stokes' words in the police reports were, "I wanted an apology, didn't get one," after he turned himself in and confessed to the shooting.

Though Stokes reportedly passed a lie detector test, Blackwell denied the allegations. The police found no actual evidence and the case was dropped. Father Blackwell was allowed to return to his duties with the stipulation that he could no longer counsel young men.

Five years after this incident, however, a second allegation of sexual abuse of a minor was made, and in 1998 Blackwell admitted he had had a five year sexual relationship with a teen-age boy. Blackwell was ousted from the church, but no criminal charges were filed in that matter.

In an interview with CNN's Connie Chung, Tamara Stokes, Dontee's mother, said her son had become increasingly upset over the stories of sex abuse in the church–to the point that he became depressed and suicidal. She suggested the news reports had affected him mentally. "He would get very upset," she said, "and he would sometimes get out of control. He was definitely in a different state of mind." On the *Today Show* she said her son "snapped."

Stokes reportedly would never "go into the details" of what actually happened between him and Blackwell. Tiffany Taft, Stokes' girlfriend and mother of his 20-month-old daughter said, "It was a touchy subject." Whatever happened, it appears to be something deeper and darker than the fondling Stokes reported in 1993. Stokes shot Blackwell with a .357-caliber magnum at close range.

Before this incident, the last time a sex scandal involving a Black priest made national news occurred nearly twenty years ago, when an allegation was made that Rev. George Stallings of Washington, D.C. was involved in a homosexual affair. In Rev. Stallings' case, however, no minors were involved and he faced no criminal charges. Rev. Stallings denied the accusation, but he eventually left the Catholic Church to form his own independent congregation.

These allegations and confirmed cases are devastating to "believers" and the faith community. They literally shake the faith of those who believe in God and his workmen, who are called and ordained by him.

It diminishes the levels of respect one has for these men and women of the cloth. It makes the job of those who are sincere very difficult. I constantly pray for Bishop Hubbard that he will "weather the storm." The scriptures teach us that "Weeping may endure for a night but joy comes in the morning" (Psalm 30.5). I hope that along with the morning light there will come healing. We pray for healing. We say to the abusing priest: Seek help for your illness. It is wrong to alienate the trust of those who blindly trust you. It is wrong to abuse your power and authority over those whom you control.

There are numerous other priests who follow that same pattern of being abusers. On the other hand, we are grateful for other priests, such as Father Peter Young and his tireless efforts to rehabilitate addicted persons.

The Catholic faith is not alone in its suffering. Acts of abuse happen in other religions. It happens in our church. Maybe not at the rate that we are currently seeing among the priests, but it happens.

As a community, we cannot judge any one group. We can only hope that this illness and this pattern do not pop up in our own churches. African Americans will suffer in silence. It will be very damaging, and many will be damaged long before the public knows.

TRUST IS THE MAJOR FACTOR

We follow man as he follows God. Perhaps it is the "idol worship" syndrome that we have that makes us believe that men of the cloth are God. So, all of the blame is not on the priests. Some of it belongs to us.

I believe at this point in time the African American community is not "pointing fingers," or "painting the priests with a broad brush," and I am not sure if it has affected us in our sending our children to Catholic schools. I believe we are prayerful for the church and all who worship–the parishioners, the victims, and the priest.

We have high regard and great respect for Bishop Hubbard. He has always been a champion for the "little guy"–the least, the last, and the lost. This was how he was as a street priest in the South End of Albany, and he has continued to live this out as a bishop. He can always be counted on to speak out against the injustices of racial discrimination, racial profiling, the death penalty, homelessness, hunger, poverty, and the war.

The Church and Gay Men:
A Spiritual Opportunity in the Wake
of the Clergy Sexual Crisis

Robert L. Miller, Jr.

SUMMARY. After examining the historic and continued experience of homophobia espoused by catechetical doctrine of the Roman Catholic Church, this article invites people who have been deeply wounded by the clergy sexual misconduct scandal to actively use spirituality to reframe their relationship with the Church. The Buddhist notion of crisis, which contains both danger and opportunity, is one of a series of lenses through which this conversation is contextualized. *[Article copies available for a fee from The Haworth Document Delivery Service: 1-800-HAWORTH. E-mail address: <docdelivery@haworthpress.com> Website: <http://www.HaworthPress.com> © 2003 by The Haworth Press, Inc. All rights reserved.]*

KEYWORDS. Homophobia and sexual abuse, homophobia and Roman Catholic Church, gay priests and sexual abuse

INTRODUCTION

I am grateful for the opportunity to contribute to this discussion. Privileging as many voices as possible in such a difficult, yet robust time in-

[Haworth co-indexing entry note]: "The Church and Gay Men: A Spiritual Opportunity in the Wake of the Clergy Sexual Crisis." Miller, Robert L. Jr. Co-published simultaneously in *Journal of Religion & Abuse* (The Haworth Pastoral Press, an imprint of The Haworth Press, Inc.) Vol. 5, No. 3, 2003, pp. 87-102; and: *Sexual Abuse in the Catholic Church: Trusting the Clergy?* (ed: Marie M. Fortune, and W. Merle Longwood) The Haworth Pastoral Press, an imprint of The Haworth Press, Inc., 2003, pp. 87-102. Single or multiple copies of this article are available for a fee from The Haworth Document Delivery Service [1-800-HAWORTH, 9:00 a.m. - 5:00 p.m. (EST). E-mail address: docdelivery@haworthpress.com].

http://www.haworthpress.com/web/JORA
© 2003 by The Haworth Press, Inc. All rights reserved.
Digital Object Identifier:10.1300/J154v05n03_13

spires hope and harkens thoughts of a stronger, more grace-filled Church.

It is important to understand the various lenses through which I contemplate and understand this topic. The first lens is the Buddhist notion of crisis, which has been popularized by the Chinese symbols of danger and opportunity. The notion of opportunity is expanded to include hope. My intention here is to offer a differing perspective on the Roman Catholic Church, gay men, and the clergy sexual misconduct scandal. The connections made among these three by the church and the media have been spurious and hurtful, constituting a profound danger for both gay men and the church. My thesis is that spirituality creates the opportunity to reframe the connections and enhances the relationship for both gay men and the church. This reframing may affect a more authentic and respectful understanding between the entities. The reframing is grounded in the necessity of individuals taking greater responsibility for their relationship with God. As individuals take greater responsibility for their relationship with God, the church, the clergy and gay men may refocus their energies on healing and productive efforts, which will certainly engender hope for the body of believers.

The second lens I use to frame my comments is my identity as an African American male social work educator, researcher, and practitioner. These identities inform my understanding of social work treatment theory. Modern social work treatment theory is organized by a belief in the value of client self-determination. This value grounds the beginning work with a client, invoking an invitation for clients to recognize their inherent right and most often the capability of deciding the right action for themselves. Included in this capability is the will to explore the meaning and impact of decisions on the part of the client decision makers. The essence of self-determination is the power to decide. Essential to this power is the freedom to make decisions and the capacity to live with the consequences of those decisions. This essay is framed in the construct of self-determination.

The third lens that informs this conversation is the immutable belief for me as a Christian Catholic African American man in Paul's letter to the Philippians, specifically the articulation that "I can do all things through Christ that strengthen me" (Phil 4:13, NIV). This passage and the others like it remind me of the rich, passionate, empowering relationship I share with God.

Reframing the relationship between gay men, the church, the sexual crimes against children and adolescents with its attending conspiracy of cover-ups and denials requires examining the relationship between the church and gay men, prior to the illuminated crimes. It also requires an examination of the church's personnel policies regarding entrance requirements for preparation for the priesthood.

THE ROMAN CATHOLIC CHURCH AND GAY MEN

The relationship between the Roman Catholic Church and gay men is complicated. To gain some insight regarding the relationship between the two, a reading of the Church's doctrine is useful. The Catechism of the Roman Catholic Church is considered to be the compendium of all Catholic doctrine regarding both faith and morals. The Pope considers it "the reference text for a catechesis renewed at the living sources of the faith" (*Catechism*, p. 3).

According to the Catechism, The Roman Catholic Church does not support the full expression of homosexual orientation and behavior between adults who are willing to engage in mutually respectful and loving, committed relationships. The church teaches that genital sexual expression between different gendered adults is only sanctioned when the adults are married. Other sexual expression is fornication, which is a sin.

The church characterizes and perceives homosexual genital expression as not the same as heterosexual genital expression. There is a particular denigration of homosexual genital expression. The church characterizes homosexual acts as "acts of grave depravity" (*Catechism*, 2357). Homosexual acts are "intrinsically disordered" (SCDF, *Persona Humana* 8). They are contrary to the natural law. They do not proceed from a genuine affective and sexual complementarity. Under no circumstances can they be approved. The church clearly condemns homosexual genital sexual expression as an activity requiring a response of prayer and penance. The Catechism teaches that homosexual persons, by the virtues of self-mastery, which leads to inner freedom, by prayer and sacramental grace and other forms of assistance, can advance toward Christian perfection (*Catechism*, 2359).

There is a specious recognition offered by the church in its teaching on homosexuality. Homosexual orientation is different than homosexual behavior that is genital homosexual expression. While the genital homosexual expression or "acts" are both "gravely depraved and intrinsically disordered," the church also recognizes that homosexual orientation is not a choice. Further, the church recognizes that living as a homosexual may be a trial (*Catechism*, 2358).

Upon reflection, if one is gay, this teaching is stunning in its assault on one's psychological, emotional and spiritual understanding of one's self. Intrinsic means belonging to a thing by its very nature. Disorder lacks order or regular arrangement; confusion is a breach of order. Depraved means corrupt, wicked or perverted. Its synonyms are debased, degenerate, dissolute, profligate, licentious, lascivious, and lewd according to the *Random House Collegiate Dictionary*.

Human development theory suggests that sexuality is central to our identity as human beings. Understanding one's gender and the sexual expression of that gender is a defining construct in one's understanding of him or herself. "Intrinsically disordered and gravely depraved" implies that the gay man's nature is corrupt. Furthermore, not only is his nature corrupt, but he is corrupt through no choice of his own, but rather an accident of birth. The images those words illicit effectively negate and potentially demolish one's ability to value his personhood. Words like "stigma," "shame," "diminished self worth," and "unworthy" are evoked from this understanding of the church's position on the homosexual person.

THE ADDED CONFUSION

While, according to the Catechism, the homosexual cannot enjoy a fully integrated genital sexual expression and life, the American Roman Catholic bishops have taught that parents should not reject their gay children. The National Conference of Catholic Bishops' statement, *Always Our Children* (1997), emphasizes that God loves every person as a unique individual and does not love him or her less because he or she is a homosexual. The tenor of the document is "demonstrating love for gay and lesbian children must be a priority among Roman Catholic parents."

Apparently, the bishops were moved to write this pastoral letter because they were made aware that parents were accepting the teaching of the church regarding homosexuality as a higher order imperative. The teaching created a position for the parents of gay children to choose between the teaching of the church and their children. The bishops' letter describes mothers and fathers suffering guilt, shame and loneliness due to the church's teaching on homosexuality. It also suggested that many youths are rejected by their families and sent into the streets. The document makes connections between parental rejection of their children and young gays and lesbians succumbing to suicidal tendencies, drug abuse and disease. So powerful is the stance of the church on homosexuality, it seems that the hierarchy was afraid that the parents were choosing the teaching of the church over the health and welfare of their children.

That the bishops were concerned enough to write the pastoral letter illuminates the pain caused by the teaching of the Catechism. They were aware that the teaching was powerful, and it threatened the natural order relationship between parents and their gay child. In the worst-case scenario, parents were sacrificing the lives of their children to remain "consistent" with the teaching of the church. Whether the stance of the church promoted castigation and called for the rejection of gay children is an argument for another time. The point remains, that the teaching of the church on homosexuality warranted a pastoral action by the American Catholic Church hierarchy. By implication, the letter was necessary to help balance the life-threatening stance of the catechetical teachings.

That parents had to be told by the hierarchy of the church not to reject their gay child suggests that the power of the teaching on homosexuality created a threat to the health and welfare of human beings because of an accident of their birth. The untold psychological, emotional and spiritual pain for both the parents and children borders on the unimaginable. Consider what parents must feel like as they felt compelled to cut off their child. The documented loss of life to disease and suicide, in addition to homelessness, and illicit behaviors that these children employed to survive on the streets is difficult to conceptualize. The reality is that we don't have to imagine it, because the data are recorded by law enforcement and federal public health agencies, namely the Centers for Disease Control and Prevention.

For the gay man who was not thrown out of his parents' home, he too confronts a confusing set of realities while attempting to remain in communion with the church. When taken in their entirety, the teachings seem difficult, if not inconsistent with his humanity. On the one hand, the church acknowledges that homosexuality is not a choice, but rather a condition to struggle with all of one's life. The church declares that homosexuality can never be approved. The homosexual person must either extinguish his homosexual genital desires or be in a constant state of repentance and in need of the rite of reconciliation. This presents a level of difficulty for two reasons. First, the gay man is apologizing for an act, which depending on the context may be a very self-generative, very natural and loving expression with another consenting adult, an act where the power and love of God can be present and affirming! Second, a question is illuminated regarding the consistency of a human being born corrupted, requiring that he engage in a psychological struggle all of his life with something that for many men is a central identity. From the perspective of social justice and honoring one's humanity, that position is violent and does not engender peace and self-love, appreciation or worth. Lastly, to ask someone to struggle with something that is so core to his identity, which is his nature, is not consistent with my understanding of a just and loving God.

The church "recognizes" that the homosexual may be engaged in a trial with his condition. Gay men should not be discriminated against and parents should love their gay children, all the while encouraging them not to engage in "unnatural acts," nor explore the possibility of genital sexual relationships or emotionally committed relationships with other men. These teachings create a conundrum regarding the healthy development of self-esteem and self worth. To say that homosexuality is a trial makes one quickly reflect on the many places, people and things that will reject a person solely because he is gay.

That the church offers a nondiscriminatory stance for gay people is important. But there is a concern whether, by teaching the intrinsic evil of such people, there is some reason why they should be discriminated against. If one is evil, then the question does arise, why should the person not be shunned? To ask people to distinguish between such shunning and discriminating requires a highly complicated level of discernment. Furthermore, to ask individuals to avoid genital sexual expression as an indication of their commitment and love for each other serves to diminish their ability to live out the fullness of their humanity. And it creates a condition where the gay man is, at best, forced to create a choice between himself and doctrines of the church, which some interpret as an extension of God's will.

THE CHURCH AS MEDIATOR

The church has positioned itself as the mediator between God and humanity. Through its precepts of divine revelation and the creation of sacramental moments, namely those outward symbols of inward graces, the "lay person" is encouraged to depend on the church for those acts, as well as other teachings. For the church to promulgate its teachings on homosexuality as God's decree, the homosexual, unless he seeks additional understanding, is left to believe and accept that these statements are how God feels about him. The ramifications of this belief transcend every facet of the homosexual man's being.

To teach that a fundamental core identity of a human being should never be accepted, in this case homosexuality, assaults his ego and cognitive structuring. It is also portends some unintended consequences. By making homosexuality something that is never to be approved, he finds himself struggling to determine if he has any self worth, which is a reasonable question given the teaching assaults his core identity. From a spiritual perspective, a condition is created that suggests that gay men can never hope to expect that they can live out their lives in peace and joy in a homosexual relationship. Nor can they expect to have their relationships blessed or sanctioned by the Roman Catholic Church. Some men may also question whether God will bless their relationship. Both of these ideas negatively impact how the gay man understands how God sees him. He feels unworthy and unlovable, or conditionally loved, and he is challenged to see his life as a gift from God. It may challenge other beliefs, namely, whether he is created in the image and likeness of God. Examples of other challenges include the gay man's prayer life, capacity or willingness to engage in mutually satisfying relationships and HIV disease prevention.

PRAYER LIFE

Praying for ourselves and each other has a beneficial effect. In order to pray, one must believe that God is in relationship with one's self. People must believe that God loves them and will hear and answer their prayers. One's experience of prayer is an indication of his or her spirituality. If the church says that certain men are born corrupt and depraved, they are less likely or able to establish a robust and personal relationship with God. In the absence of a relationship with God, they are less likely to use spirituality as a healing agent.

SAME SEX RELATIONSHIPS

The social science literature describes difficulties some gay men have with self-esteem, namely their willingness and ability to feel good about themselves, and their capacity to entertain the possibility of long term healthy relationships with other men. The natural longing and yearning to be in intimate, life giving, full relationships is significantly challenged. There are behavioral health ramifications as well.

SPIRITUALITY AND HIV DISEASE

The HIV disease literature indicates research findings on the efficacy of spirituality and a relationship with God have as healing agents in people's lives. As a social work researcher examining how gay men cope while living with AIDS, I have been particularly interested in the role of spirituality as a coping strategy for such men. My clinical practice is multi-ethnic, -racial and -cultural. Through my research, I have found that black gay men who use spirituality as a coping strategy while living with AIDS have a personal relationship with God and have come to understand that God loves them as gay men (Miller, 2000). Moreover, they conceptualize their sexual orientation as a gift from God, which they use to create peace and healing for themselves and other people (Miller, 2000).

Additionally, other research indicates a relationship between spirituality and HIV prevention efforts. In spite of the current availability of powerful, life prolonging drugs for HIV disease, there is no cure. Consequently, prevention is the most effective combatant to HIV disease.

Robert and Mindy Fullilove of the Columbia University Community Research Group highlight the factors that impede effective HIV prevention messages.

> The messages of God's unwillingness to be present [in] the sexual lives of gay men creates a sense of dislocation from a spiritual life and a faith community because of one's self was found wanting and was deeply depressing. This also produced a loss of self-esteem. Some men are so disoriented by their experiences of stigma, both in the Church and in the general community; they do not feel empowered to care for themselves. Such feelings can undermine the individual's ability to practice safe sex, seek medical care in a timely fashion, or follow other health practices essential to well being. (1999, p. 1127)

For gay men who are at risk for HIV disease or living with AIDS, to be bereft of spirituality as a coping strategy and potential healing agent for a deadly disease is unjust and inconsistent with the direct messages of Jesus Christ. I submit that depriving men of a healing opportunity is an unintended, though no less deleterious, consequence of the teaching of the church regarding homosexuality.

My point is that the church's relationship with gay men, prior to the illuminated crimes against children and adolescents, has been hurtful and arguably life threatening to the gay man's well-being. The historical relationship between the church and gay men has been difficult. In addition, the reaction by the church regarding gay men in the wake of the clergy sexual offenses and the conspiracy of cover up has been astounding.

INSULT TO INJURY:
LAYING THE SEXUAL MISCONDUCT SCANDAL
AT THE FEET OF GAY PRIESTS

The clergy sexual misconduct scandal is both deceptively simple and profoundly complicated, and it requires courage and strength to see clearly through an array of emotions and facts. We are painfully aware that the first victims of these crimes were minors, both children and adolescents, who are now adults, and we want them to have justice and healing. We also see their families as being victimized by the church. Other victims are the congregants whose pastors were named as perpetrators of the sexual crimes against minors. Their shock and feelings of betrayal and loss are significant. To know that the man you confessed to, the man who initiated transubstantiation on your behalf, baptized your children, married them, and buried your parents, relatives, and friends was a violent criminal is deeply disturbing. Yet you also believe that if these alleged crimes can be substantiated, the perpetrator needs to be held accountable for his offenses.

We can surely understand that men who sexually abuse children and adolescents, though they must be held accountable for their deeds, are also in need of treatment. What is less clear and requires more insight are the actions of the bishops and cardinals who engaged in conspiracies to protect their priest personnel, which in many cases, created opportunities for additional abuse in other parishes. We have heard several responses to this query, and they center on the statement, "It is less than useful to judge past performance by today's standards." I will leave the merits of that argument for the reader to debate. However, what is less arguable is that hundreds of thousands of people, including gay men, have been hurt in a pernicious manner by the hierarchy's handling of the clergy sexual misconduct scandal.

It is also important to understand that when *most* gay men talk about and refer to homosexual emotional and genital relationships, they are not referring to minors, but to their peers who can make informed choices. As Groth and Gary (1982) suggest, "the research to date all points to there being no significant relationship between a homosexual lifestyle and child molestation" (p. 147). Furthermore, Dr. Nathaniel McConaghy (1998) cautions against confusing homosexuality with pedophilia. He noted, "The man who offends against prepubertal or immediately postpubertal boys is typically not sexually interested in older men or in women" (p. 259).

Most credible data sources report the majority of the victims of clergy sexual misconduct were adolescents, not children. The clergy most often victimized adolescent boys. It is important to note here that an adult man having sexual relationships with minors of either gender is a crime. While there are discussions about the age at which an adolescent is competent to make a decision regarding participation in sexual activities with adult men, the adult man universally has the obligation to exert his authority and power on behalf of the adolescent, refraining from sex with the adolescent.

I define homosexuality as same gender affections, genital expression, social and political thought and action. In addition, I regard the notion of homosexual relationships as normatively occurring between two consenting age-appropriate peers. To cast the conversation in any other light is inaccurate. While there are men who engage in sexual activities with minors, that activity is not typically engaged in by well-adjusted gay men.

Given that well-adjusted homosexuals want to engage in respectful, mutually life giving relationships with their peers, it is inaccurate to portray the clergy sexual abuse between adult men and minors as homosexual activity in the same way that most homosexual men conduct themselves. The sexual exploitation of children and adolescents by Fr. John Geoghan and others like him is more consistent with pederasty, which has no bearing upon nor does it resemble anything that most gay men intentionally seek. The differences between those two behaviors in their different contexts cannot be overstated.

Therefore, assertions that the clergy sexual assaults are intricately related to the presence of gay male priests among the clergy requires an honest and accurate assessment. What transpired between the clergy and the minors is best described as activities involving the victims and the perpetrators of the crimes. Objectively, what can be said is that adult males (priests) participated in genital sexual relationships (the extent of which varies considerably according to each case) with minors, most of whom were male adolescents. To make any generalizations from the objective facts in the absence of in-depth research would produce erroneous assertions. It perpetuates an inauthentic understanding of homosexuality and its relationship to the criminal activity perpetrated by priests and kept secret by their bishops.

However, the church does not concur. In addition to the policy developed by the Bishops' Conference in Dallas, in 2002, providing a formalized procedure for local bishops to hold clergy perpetrators accountable for their offenses, the Vatican, through its Congregation of Bishops and Congregation for Divine Worship, has begun discussions on the merits of making homosexuality a reason to deny entrance to seminary and ultimately declaring that gay men should be banned from ordination to the priesthood. In December, 2002, Cardinal Jorge Arturo Medina Estevez, the prefect for the Congregation for Divine Worship and the Discipline of the Sacraments, published a letter declaring that gay men and men with same-sex tendencies should not be ordained as priests (Tallahassee.com). This opinion, while not yet a directive, is being considered as an employment policy requirement for men desiring to become priests. Many consider the opinion as an indication of the direction of the Vatican regarding gay men in the priesthood. This is not a new stance; it first appeared in 1961. The Sacred Congregation for Religious published a document stating, "Those affected by the perverse inclination of homosexuality or pederasty should be excluded from religious vows and ordination, because priestly ministry would place such persons in grave danger" (S.C.Rel., 1961).

While there are many things gravely injurious about this proposed policy, what is most striking is its lack of focus regarding the issue at hand. To suggest that a corrective action to prevent the criminal sexual behavior of priests against children and adolescents is to ban all homosexuals from the priesthood may or may not yield the intended result, namely a cadre of priest clergy who all share a heterosexual orientation and are free from desires to have sex with minors. How the church would enforce the directive, as well as what it would do regarding all of the current priests who are gay and actively carrying out their priestly duties, is another question. My concern is the emotional and psychological violence the message will convey. Gay men who love God with their whole heart, mind, and souls, who want to dedicate their lives to priestly ministry in the church, would be told the gifts they have to offer are less of a concern than their potential to engage in pedophilic or ephebophilic activity as a clergy member. In fact, the not-so-subtle message is, if you are gay and ordained you will likely engage in sexual crimes with children and adolescents. It is difficult to understand what is reasonable about this assertion, and it vividly illuminates the continued assault on gay men by the Catholic Church.

At this point, I have hopefully made plain the articulated position of the Roman Catholic Church regarding gay men. From its source documents, gay men are considered corrupt, evil, and disordered. They are not allowed any genital expression of their sexual orientation or to establish a mutually respectful and loving relationship with another man. At best they are encouraged to live a celibate life.

The church does recognize that parents of gay children should love them and not reject them. The church also teaches that homosexuals should not be discriminated against. The irony of this last statement cannot be ignored. Gay men should not be discriminated against, that is unless they seek entrance into the priesthood. In that instance, however, it is a matter of policy to discriminate against gay men, denying them entrance into training for priesthood. The church is actively reaffirming its policy of banning gay men from entering the priesthood.

THE OPPORTUNITY AND THE HOPE

I began this article describing the various lenses through which I have come to contemplate this topic, the first of which is the Buddhist notion of Crisis, which is the combination of danger and opportunity. The church is in a crisis, of which clergy sexual misconduct is but one indication of its dangers. The greater danger the church finds itself centers in the dependence it creates for its believers. The church teaches its members that sacramental moments, those outward symbols of inward graces, can only be offered by the clergy.

Upon deeper reflection, a sacramental moment is time and space where we consciously evoke the presence of God in our lives. During the times of marriage or baptism, these moments are the public blessings solicited *by clergy from God for the believers*. We, the laity, have sanctioned those men, who are ordained, to perform these acts for us. Jesus tells us, where two or three are gathered, in his name, he is there (Matthew 18:20 NIV). By yielding our authority and ability to offer public blessings solicited *by ourselves from God for ourselves*, we have abdicated our ability and responsibility for knowing God for ourselves in intimate and sacramental, life giving ways. At the very least, we have forfeited an opportunity to own our priestly identity.

If we believe that God created us in God's likeness and image, why would we think that our Creator would not be available to us whenever we needed or wanted God? By extension, why then would we not be able to create our own sacramental moments, namely those times when we needed God to be present in the place of our condition at that time? This question is not to suggest that the sacramental moments that the Church offers are not important, because they are. However, I am suggesting that there is an additional perspective in relation to how outward symbols of inwards graces are conveyed. I am suggesting that as human beings created by God, and redeemed by Jesus Christ, we have the capacity and obligation to make our relationship with God our Creator personal and intimate. We have an obligation to the one that created us to know our Creator for ourselves, using other data sources such as the Catechism of the Roman Catholic Church as additional sources of information but not as the primary source of understanding our relationship with God, for example. As creations of God, we are the primary source of knowledge of God's love, care and thinking for us and about us. We can look to other sources like the church, its catechism and clergy, but we have an obligation first to seek God for ourselves and to know and love God, however, we conceptualize God.

Though this stance might sound radical, it evokes a personal responsibility for the quality of relationship between God and us. It also creates a different paradigm regarding who has the most knowledge about what God thinks and feels about us. This stance is an important consideration for the gay man. It is not reasonable nor is it consistent for people to be told that they should struggle all of their lives. I concede I am not a biblical scholar; however, in my reading of the Bible, the various events that show God's love for humanity do not insist that people accept a struggle for the balance of their lives.[1] From a place of justice and love, human beings have the right to peace and fulfillment. The gay man is also worthy and deserving of peace and love. As a matter of doctrine, for any number of reasons, the Church seems unwilling to acknowledge publicly our individual capacity to know God for ourselves, with the same energy it has castigated the gay man's genital sexual expression. However, the effects create danger for gay men and those who love them.

From a place of self-determination, a gay man has a decision to make. He can decide to languish in a catechetical stance that does not affirm the dignity of his humanity, or he can utilize all of the gifts of his creation and explore for himself, the questions, "Does God really love me in the totality of my creation? What does that mean? How do I know?"

There comes a time when human beings must confront truth in their lives. We have to understand what informs that truth. We must come to understand that there are various sources for information and data. If we have some concept of God and believe in God, then it is reasonable to ask if what others have said about God is consistent with our personal lived experiences of God. While I do not want to underestimate the importance of living with creeds and norms of behaviors, it is not reasonable nor loving to ask people to accept a creed that is antithetical to and inconsistent with their core experience if it is not their nature.

Paul's articulation to the Philippians, "I can do all things through Christ that strengthens me (Philippians 4:13 NIV) includes having a personal, direct relationship with God. As an African American man who loves God, I choose to organize my life around those scriptures that support my belief. When challenged, my relationships with God and Jesus are validated through a review of my life history and the songs and hymns of my faith–"Blessed Assurance," "Great Is Thy Faithfulness," "Come Thou Fount of Every Blessing," "Come Ye Disconsolate," and "When We all Get to Heaven"–as well as those works arranged and composed by Leon C. Roberts,[2] to name a few.

Finally, the opportunity for all of us in the wake of the clergy scandal is a reexamination of a direct, loving and reciprocal communication with God. Moreover, we can begin to own our relationship with God and discern what God is asking of us. If we take greater ownership of our relationship with God, we can reframe our relationship with the church and the clergy. By becoming more intimate with God, we become more aware of how God works in our lives. We then become the expert of God's presence in our lives.

This position then allows us to reframe our relationship with the church. Instead of it being the primary source of data about God, it becomes an additional source of understanding. From a post-modern perspective, having many sources of information about God, we have the opportunity to experience a relationship that has depth and texture. Ultimately, by shifting the responsibility of our relationship with God to ourselves, we create two results. The first is that we become more intimate with God and become a credible witness to the world regarding the love of God in our lives. The second is that the church is relieved of the obligation of being the sole source of determining when God is going be present. In effect, we, along with the church, engage in creating sacramental moments. In so doing, we, as laity, become powerful witnesses to the church and the clergy as they learn from our lived experiences the manifold ways God can be present. We also can inform the church that some of the positions that it has taught and continues to teach are inconsistent with our lived experiences as God's creatures.

This reframing allows those men and women who have been diminished by the church because of some characteristic that is not in their control to experience fully the gift of their creation. Honoring the gift creates a teachable moment for the church. This is true for the gay man. Such a moment is growth. Growth is a powerful testament to God's gift of life to us.

The crisis of the clergy sexual misconduct is another indication that the church itself is still growing in grace and wisdom. We, the laity, have an important opportunity to be thoughtful, prayerful, and honest as we hold the church in love and mercy while insisting that the hierarchy is accountable for the crimes committed by some clergy and bishops. In this place of opportunity and hope, we too have the obligation to assume our rightful position as conscious, loving human beings capable of direct communication with God in our lives. It is by assuming our intentional and purposeful relationship with God that we can stand ready to assist the church as it continues to live the revelations that all creation yearn to bring forth. This is true for parents of children and adolescents who were victimized as well as for gay men and women. We can call forth justice and we can stand in the place where it meets mercy and grace. Together, with an adult faith, we can create an outward symbol of inward graces. That sacramental moment is an opportunity that creates hope for us all.

NOTES

1. This discussion of struggle is not the same as the notion of redemptive suffering offered in the book of Isaiah. Redemptive suffering is associated with a greater good. To struggle against yourself because of a natural sexual orientation produces no greater good, only psychological, emotional, and spiritual pain.

2. "Blessed Assurance" was written by Fanny J. Crosby and music by Mrs. Joseph F. Knapp; "Great is Thy Faithfulness" was written by Thomas Chisholm and music by William M. Runyan; "Come Thou Fount of Every Blessing" was written by Robert Robinson and music by John Wyeth; and "When We All Get To Heaven" was written by Eliza Hewitt and music by Emily Wilson. The work of liturgist and composer Leon C. Roberts, who died in 1999, is published through Oregon Catholic Press and Gregorian Institute of America.

REFERENCES

Catechism of the Catholic Church. (1994). Chicago, IL: Loyola University Press.

Fullilove, M.T., and R.E. (1999). "Stigma as an Obstacle to AIDS Action: The case of the African American Community." *American Behavioral Scientist*, Vol. 42, No. 7. April, 1117-1127.

Groth, A.N., & Gary, T.S. (1982). "Heterosexuality, homosexuality, and pedophilia: Sexual offenses against children and adult sexual orientation." In A.M. Scacco (Ed.), *Male Rape: A Casebook Of Sexual Aggressions* (pp. 143-152). New York: AMS Press.

Holy Bible. New International Version. (1978). Grand Rapids: Zondervan Bible Publishers.

McConaghy, N. (1998). "Pedophilia: A review of the evidence." *Australian and New Zealand Journal of Psychiatry,* 32(2), 252-265

Miller, Jr., R.L. (2000). "The meaning and utility of Spirituality in the Lives of African American Gay Men living with AIDS." Unpublished dissertation.

National Conference of Catholic Bishops. (1997). *Always Our Children: A Pastoral Message to Parents of Homosexual Children and Suggestions for Pastoral Ministers.* A national statement of the NCCB Committee on Marriage and Family. Monsignor Dennis M. Schnurr, General Secretary. Washington, DC: United States Catholic Conference.

Sacred Congregation for the Religious. *Careful Selection And Training Of Candidates For The States Of Perfection And Sacred Orders* (S. C. Rel., 2 Feb., 1961).

Sacred Congregation for the Doctrine of the Faith (SCDF). (1975). *Persona Humana–Declaration On Certain Questions Concerning Sexual Ethics.*

Tallahassee.com, Nicole Winfield, Associated Press, December 5, 2002.

Conclusion

Marie M. Fortune

This collection of articles addressing sexual abuse by Roman Catholic priests begins to bring together disparate but committed voices with a common concern to address sexual abuse in the church. As such it creates a dialogue of thoughtful authors attempting to bring some clarity and leadership to the chaos of the institutional response to the increasing disclosure of sexual abuse by priests (oftentimes committed 20-30 years ago). This is exactly what is needed at this moment.

There are concrete suggestions that deserve attention:

- Michael J. Bland suggests making the Bishops Ad Hoc Committee a standing committee. "I suggest that after being in existence for nearly 20 years the Bishops Ad Hoc Committee on Sexual Abuses needs to be recognized as a permanent committee of the Unites States Conference of Catholic Bishops. There is nothing Ad Hoc about sexual abuse." This suggestion recognizes that this is not a momentary crisis but a long term one and we need dioceses available and open to training and strategizing. Bland quotes T. S. Eliot: "We had the experience, but missed the meaning." Reflection on the meaning of all this is the only way to learn from it.
- Bishop Hubbard brought the refreshing breath of air when he acknowledged the responsibility of the institution for creation of this mess: "There is the two-fold scandal of the breach of sacred trust

[Haworth co-indexing entry note]: "Conclusion." Fortune, Marie M. Co-published simultaneously in *Journal of Religion & Abuse* (The Haworth Pastoral Press, an imprint of The Haworth Press, Inc.) Vol. 5, No. 3, 2003, pp. 103-106; and: *Sexual Abuse in the Catholic Church: Trusting the Clergy?* (ed: Marie M. Fortune, and W. Merle Longwood) The Haworth Pastoral Press, an imprint of The Haworth Press, Inc., 2003, pp. 103-106. Single or multiple copies of this article are available for a fee from The Haworth Document Delivery Service [1-800-HAWORTH, 9:00 a.m. - 5:00 p.m. (EST). E-mail address: docdelivery@haworthpress.com].

http://www.haworthpress.com/web/JORA
© 2003 by The Haworth Press, Inc. All rights reserved.
Digital Object Identifier: 10.1300/J154v05n03_14

by individual priests and the way bishops like myself have mis-handled such misconduct, because of ignorance, fear or the mis-guided attempt to protect the church from scandal. Indeed, as Fr. Cozzens has noted, this moral ineptitude in giving greater priority to the church's image than to the protection of children has now become the scandal." This self-awareness and recognition of re-sponsibility at the administrative level is absolutely critical to change in the way these cases are handled. Bishop Hubbard went on to say: "Here I believe is where the National Review Board, chaired by former Oklahoma Governor Frank Keating, can make an enormous contribution by ascertaining these figures, and any diocesan bishop who does not comply should be subject to censure or removal." As of this writing, Governor Keating has resigned from the National Review Board after confronting the stonewall-ing by some bishops.

Bishop Hubbard highlighted the importance of research: "I be-lieve the National Review Board can make an enormous contribu-tion by commissioning scientific research on the data it compiles. Catholics and other members of the public have raised legitimate questions about the underlying causes of sexual abuse by clergy. These questions deserve answers based on careful research, not anecdotal evidence or preconceived assumptions." (Dr. Newberger's article is an excellent summary of what we know clinically about sex abusers.)

- Archbishop Flynn raised the important point that yes, media ac-counts often fail to provide context about where and when the problem occurred, how it was handled and what has been done or is being done to address it. "For example, should current knowledge of 'best practices' necessarily be the standard for determining legal liability for decisions made 20 or 30 years ago; or if liability is conceded how does one assess the mone-tary compensation? Even among professionals in the field there is plenty of room for reasonable disagreement about how much even a just claim is worth." This is a hard issue. We didn't know then what we know now. But one would have hoped that the overriding pastoral concern would have motivated a bishop to seek help and consultation based on common sense and protec-tion of children.

- Fr. Cozzens did not hesitate to support the work of the Commis-sion. "Catholics are watching to see if the United States Confer-ence of Bishops will give the Keating Commission the on-going financial support and cooperation it needs to fulfill its mandate of insuring the norms of the Dallas meeting are followed." He also did not hesitate to challenge the sometimes paranoid response of bishops to the media coverage: "My point is that we are giving ammunition to our enemies when we are not candid and forthcoming about the present scandal."

Of course, as non-Catholics it is our responsibility to keep the whole picture before us, acknowledging that every faith tradition is struggling with this issue of abuse by clergy. In this way we can help to create space for Catholics to have an open and honest discussion without fear of retaliation by the non-Catholic community.

- Finally Cozzens affirmed the importance of lay involvement in the solution to this crisis: "Lay women and men, of course, like their ordained conferees, are both saints and sinners, subject to the same human weaknesses we now see so clearly in clergy and other church leaders. They seem, nonetheless, to be anointed at this precarious juncture in the church's history to offer the leadership and vision so wanting in many of our ecclesial assemblies. They deserve to be heard, respected, and encouraged. I believe they are God's gift to our troubled churches."

This is probably the most important antidote to this long and painful history of mismanagement of sexual abuse by priests. This is also why the response of some bishops to groups like Voice of the Faithful has been disappointing. Denying concerned lay people the opportunity to meet on church property does not send a message of openness and dialogue to the wider church.

- Alomar, Pope, and Miller expand the discussion even further and emphasize the double impact of clergy abuse within communities of color and the gay and lesbian community. As always, the more marginalized people are, the more they experience the fall-out from these kinds of institutional crises. But their insights and leadership are also invaluable in the overall discussion of responses and the future.

Unfortunately there have been some who suggest that it's time to move on from this "crisis" in order to get back to the *real* work of the church. Yet again this betrays a lack of understanding of what this is all about. At this moment in history, addressing sexual abuse by priests *is* the real work of the church–not the *only* work, but real nonetheless. The "least of these" have finally found their voices and are demanding justice and change from their own church. They are faithful Catholics who believe all that they were taught over the years, and they expect their church to listen and to be the church.

There was a film released in 2003 called *Whale Rider*. It is a New Zealand film about a young girl in line to be chief of her people but passed over by the elders because she is female. Yet she clearly has the gifts necessary for leadership: vision, courage, insight, commitment, and a deep desire to save her culture and its people. The stubborn denial of her leadership in spite of all the signs to the contrary jeopardizes the community's future. Something is clearly wrong, out-of-sync. Yet the hard headedness of the patriarch of the clan persists. Finally a crisis reveals the young girl's gifts and calling, and the community, along with the elder, move to affirm her and follow her. Perhaps this is an apt film metaphor for the Roman Catholic Church in the US to consider at this moment in history. The leadership that is needed to move forward and bring healing may come from unexpected places.

Index

© 2003 by The Haworth Press, Inc. All rights reserved.

BOOK ORDER FORM!

Order a copy of this book with this form or online at:
http://www.haworthpress.com/store/product.asp?sku=5171

Sexual Abuse in the Catholic Church

Trusting the Clergy?

_____ in softbound at $17.95 (ISBN: 0-7890-2465-9)
_____ in hardbound at $29.95 (ISBN: 0-7890-2464-0)

COST OF BOOKS _____	❑**BILL ME LATER:** Bill-me option is good on US/Canada/ Mexico orders only; not good to jobbers, wholesalers, or subscription agencies.
POSTAGE & HANDLING _____ US: $4.00 for first book & $1.50 for each additional book Outside US: $5.00 for first book & $2.00 for each additional book.	❑**Signature** _____
	❑**Payment Enclosed: $** _____
SUBTOTAL _____	❑ **PLEASE CHARGE TO MY CREDIT CARD:**
In Canada: add 7% GST. _____	❑ Visa ❑MasterCard ❑AmEx ❑Discover ❑Diner's Club ❑Eurocard ❑ JCB
STATE TAX _____ CA, IL, IN, MN, NY, OH & SD residents please add appropriate local sales tax.	**Account #** _____
FINAL TOTAL _____ If paying in Canadian funds, convert using the current exchange rate, UNESCO coupons welcome.	**Exp Date** _____ **Signature** _____ (Prices in US dollars and subject to change without notice.)

PLEASE PRINT ALL INFORMATION OR ATTACH YOUR BUSINESS CARD

Name

Address

City   State/Province   Zip/Postal Code

Country

Tel   Fax

E-Mail

May we use your e-mail address for confirmations and other types of information? ❑Yes ❑No We appreciate receiving
your e-mail address. Haworth would like to e-mail special discount offers to you, as a preferred customer.
We will never share, rent, or exchange your e-mail address. We regard such actions as an invasion of your privacy.

Order From Your **Local Bookstore** or Directly From
The Haworth Press, Inc. 10 Alice Street, Binghamton, New York 13904-1580 • USA
Call Our toll-free number (1-800-429-6784) / Outside US/Canada: (607) 722-5857
Fax: 1-800-895-0582 / Outside US/Canada: (607) 771-0012
E-mail your order to us: orders@haworthpress.com

For orders outside US and Canada, you may wish to order through your local
sales representative, distributor, or bookseller.
For information, see http://haworthpress.com/distributors

(Discounts are available for individual orders in US and Canada only, not booksellers/distributors.)

Please photocopy this form for your personal use.
www.HaworthPress.com

BOF04